PUFFIN

THE ULTIMATE GUIDE TO MONEY

THE ULTIMATE GUIDE TO MONEY

EMMANUEL ASUQUO
ILLUSTRATED BY SELOM SUNU

PUFFIN

PUFFIN BOOKS

UK | USA | Canada | Ireland | Australia
India | New Zealand | South Africa

Puffin Books is part of the Penguin Random House group of companies whose addresses can be found at global.penguinrandomhouse.com.

www.penguin.co.uk   www.puffin.co.uk   www.ladybird.co.uk

Penguin Random House UK

First published 2024
001

Text copyright © Emmanuel Asuquo, 2024
Illustrations copyright © Selom Sunu, 2024
All brands mentioned in this book are trademarks belonging to third parties.

The moral right of the author has been asserted

Text design by Dynamo Limited

Printed in Great Britain
A CIP catalogue record for this book is available from the British Library
The authorized representative in the EEA is Penguin Random House Ireland, Morrison Chambers, 32 Nassau Street, Dublin D02 YH68

ISBN: 978–0–241–64155–2

All correspondence to:
Puffin Books, Penguin Random House Children's
One Embassy Gardens, 8 Viaduct Gardens, London SW11 7BW

MIX
Paper | Supporting responsible forestry
FSC® C018179

Penguin Random House is committed to a sustainable future for our business, our readers and our planet. This book is made from Forest Stewardship Council® certified paper.

CONTENTS

INTRODUCTION	1
CHAPTER 1: MONEY, MONEY, MONEY	7
CHAPTER 2: LET THE GAMES BEGIN!	29
CHAPTER 3: TIME TO MAKE A GRAND	51
CHAPTER 4: STUNT OR SAVE	67
CHAPTER 5: THERE'S NO PLACE LIKE HOME	85
CHAPTER 6: SHOW ME THE MONEY!	105
CHAPTER 7: SO, YOU WANT TO BE A MILLIONAIRE?	129
CHAPTER 8: WHAT'S NEXT?	147
CONCLUSION	157
GLOSSARY	160

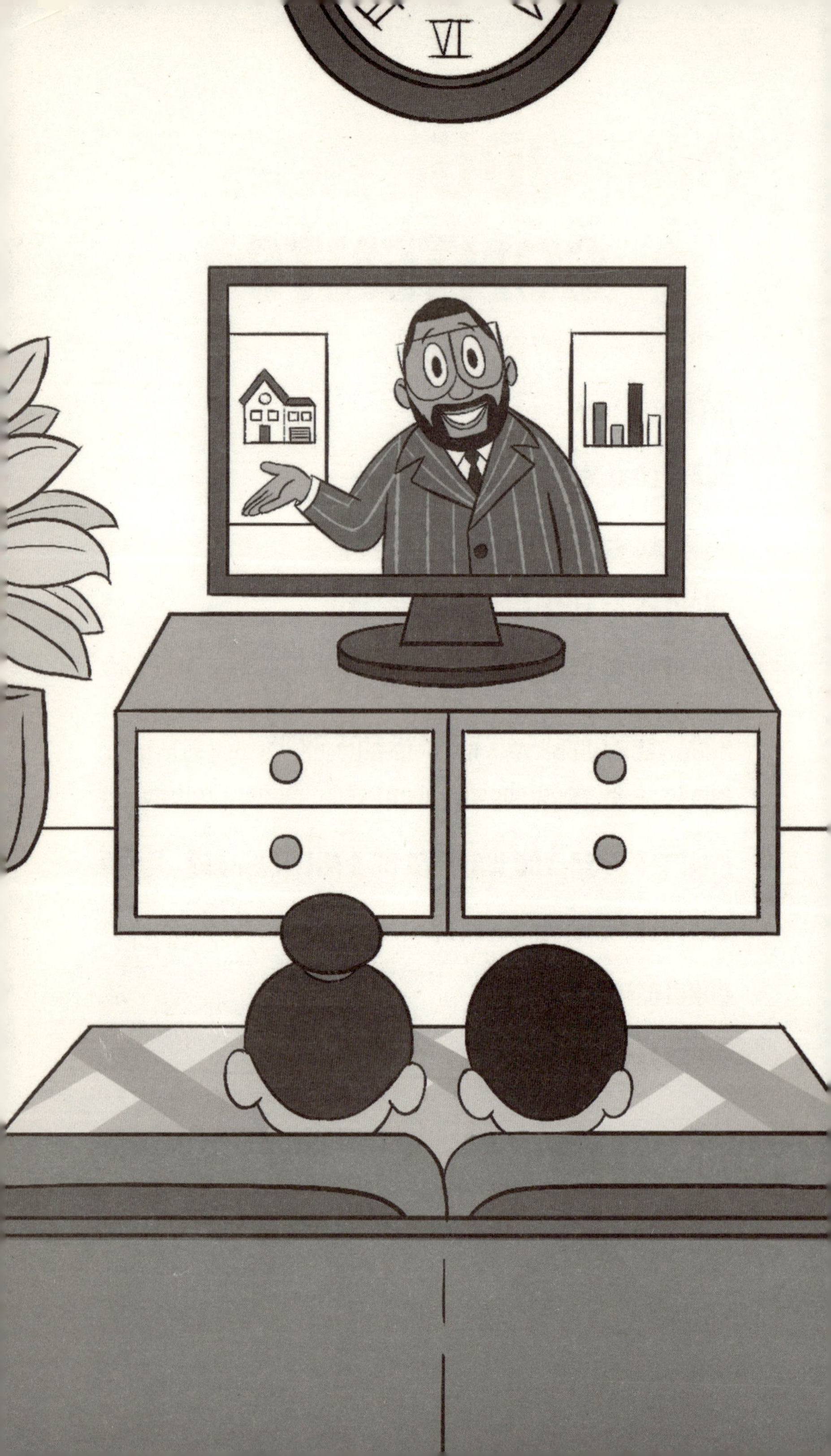

INTRODUCTION

Hello! Welcome! Nice to meet you! Let me guess: you've picked up this book because you're keen to learn about money, so you thought this might be a good place to start? Or maybe you just want to know the secret to making a million pounds? Well, that's impressive. I was nowhere near as savvy as you when I was your age.

Excuse my manners. Allow me to introduce myself. My name is Emmanuel Asuquo, but you can call me Eman (that's E-man) for short. I'm a **MONEY MAN** a.k.a a **financial advisor**. As a financial advisor, it's my job to help people make good choices about their money. You might have even seen me on the telly talking about money and helping people work out how to spend it, save it and grow it. But don't worry if you haven't because this book contains all the lessons you need to become a money master.

When I look back at my school days, some of the stuff I was taught was useful. But there were also some things that I have, personally, never used since. Like pi, and I ain't talking shepherd's or apple (it's a maths thing)! Or the elements of the periodic table. Or how to analyse every single word in a poem.

Anyway, I learned a lot at school, but I learned *nothing* about **finance**. Not a single thing. And that bugs me. In fact, it bugs me so much, I have spent much of my career teaching people all the things about money and finance that I think we should all know but aren't taught.

And recently I started to wonder, why wait until people are grown up? What if people started learning about finance when they were younger? And that led me to writing this book for *you*!

Before we begin, **LET ME TELL YOU A LITTLE BIT ABOUT MYSELF.** I was born in Tower Hamlets in East London to Nigerian parents. I wasn't the best in school academically, and – I'll be honest – sometimes that knocked my confidence and made me feel like I would never be successful. But there was one thing I was always great at and that was sport! I also had great parents and an inspirational PE teacher who encouraged me to believe in myself. With their support, I achieved the grades I needed to make it to university, where I studied accounting and finance.

While I was studying, I worked part time in a bank as a cashier, where I would help people pay money into, or take money out of, their **bank accounts** (we'll talk about what all of this means later in the book).

INTRODUCTION

This experience taught me a lot about finance that I didn't know before, and I even found myself using things I'd learned in my maths lessons in real life (except pi . . . **I'VE NEVER USED PI!**).

After I graduated from university, I became a financial advisor at the age of twenty-two. In fact, not to brag, but I was the youngest financial advisor in the country! I was really proud of myself, and it showed me that we can all do well if we work hard and believe in ourselves.

A few years later, I married my beautiful wife, and we now have four amazing kids together. This is where things changed. Don't get me wrong, I loved working as a financial advisor, but after ten years in the role, I was ready for something new. I found myself spending a lot of time having meetings with people who already had loads of money, giving them advice on how to get even more of it! And it didn't feel fair, especially since people from backgrounds like mine didn't have access to financial advice because they couldn't afford to pay for these meetings. This meant they didn't have the opportunity to learn **HOW TO GROW THEIR MONEY**.

I felt like I had to do something about it, so I decided to start my own business and share the knowledge I had gained over the years with more people.

I tried to make it affordable for everyone, regardless of where they came from. And it was a great success! I stopped working in a bank and turned my **side hustle** into my main job. Fast forward to now, and I regularly give talks about money at different events and on various TV programmes, teaching people how to save, spend and grow their money in the best way possible.

And now I want to help you!

Like I said, I struggled with some subjects at school. So I didn't want to write a book just explaining all of the confusing words out there about money and finance, because if kid Eman was reading this he would definitely get BORED and just close the book. Instead we're going to play a game, and along the way, as well as having some fun and making some cash (well, fake cash), we're going to learn loads about money and banks and **interest rates** and **inflation** and **shares** and . . . OK, I'll stop there because I can feel you drifting off already. But the point is we're going to learn all about these things within a game.

So, what game are we playing? Well . . .

We're going to be turning £1 into £1,000,000!

INTRODUCTION

(Confused by all those zeros? Don't worry, six zeros means a million!)

> **DISCLAIMER!**
>
> I live in the UK, so I've used £1 throughout the book, but you can substitute this for whatever currency your country uses.

Sounds impossible, I know, but it's not. I'm not saying it's going to be easy – if it was, we'd probably all be millionaires by now! It will take time, and in each chapter, we're going to break the journey down into small goals. Then the goals will get bigger and **BIGGER** and **BIGGER** as we move through the book.

As well as having fun, I hope you will be able to take everything you learn from the game into the real world too. And who knows – maybe you'll be able to use the lessons from this book to become a real-life millionaire one day!

Are you ready?

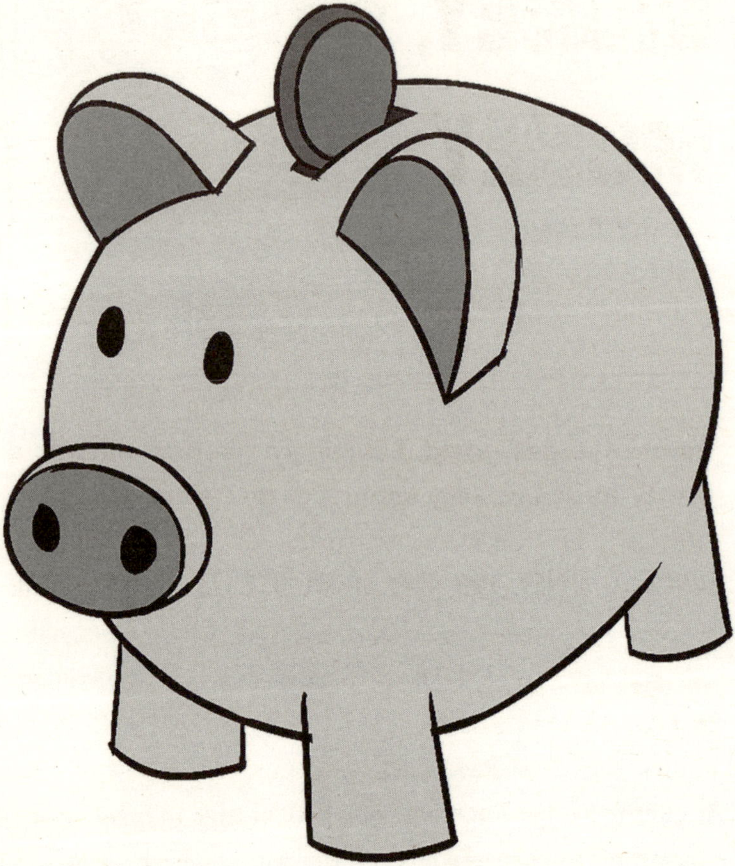

CHAPTER 1
MONEY, MONEY, MONEY

Before we get going, I think we need to answer a pretty basic but very important question.

WHAT IS MONEY AND WHY DO WE USE IT? I mean, think about it – what's it really all about? Why do we have coins and bits of paper with people's faces on them and why are they worth so much? I've got a button on my coat that's a similar size to a pound coin, but no one seems to want that in exchange for anything. So, what's the deal with money? And why do we need it?

Think back to the earliest years of your life that you can remember. When all you wished for was a toy or a game or a book, and a simple lollipop would be the highlight of your day. Don't even get me started on the joys of a Happy Meal! That would make my entire week!

THE ULTIMATE GUIDE TO MONEY

Even now, it can seem like magic when you wake up on your birthday and there it is: the exact thing you wanted, all wrapped up and waiting for you to rip into it. Ah, good times.

But the thing is, those gifts and treats **DON'T JUST APPEAR BY MAGIC**. They are yours because someone has spent their money on them. Their cash, their dollars, their bread, their bees and honey. (That last one is what we call it in East London. Why? Well, say it out loud . . . what does 'honey' rhyme with?) But you get my drift: they spent their coins to get you that gift! And it's not just gifts that cost money. In fact, most things do. Money is all around us. Most days you get dressed, travel to school, use pens and paper, and maybe watch TV. All of these things have to be paid for with money – the clothes, the transport, the stationery and the electricity. Without money, you wouldn't have or be able to use or do any of these things.

You see, our world is built around this thing called an **economy**. I know this sounds complicated, but it's actually pretty straightforward. An economy is the way that people spend and make money, which is usually by either buying or selling products or services. This means that any time we buy a product (such as food, clothing or a game) or use a service (such as taking a bus or getting a haircut) we typically owe someone money. These actions of buying and selling are what form an economy.

MONEY, MONEY, MONEY

Money tells us how much things are worth, how much wealth we have and what we can (or can't) afford to buy. This is why money is so important: it's the way we get the things we need. Without it, life can be very hard, as money is needed to have somewhere to live, pay for water and electricity, buy food, use the internet, buy new clothes and do the fun things that we enjoy. Money isn't the key to happiness, but it certainly makes everyday life much easier if we have enough to meet our basic needs.

But there was a time when people didn't use money at all. **SHOCKING, I KNOW!**

THE WORLD BEFORE MONEY

Before the days of gold coins and glossy notes – before we could spend money online or with the simple tap of a bank card – people would **barter**, or in other words, swap one thing for another. Bartering was the main way **PEOPLE WOULD EXCHANGE GOODS AND SERVICES** up until about 3,000 years ago. For example, imagine you have an apple tree, but you don't have anything to store the apples in when they're ready. The good news is your neighbour makes baskets. You could offer to give them some apples in return for one of their baskets. This is a fair exchange as it leaves you both happy – you don't have to juggle your apples any more because you've got a basket and they get a tasty treat!

This, my friends, is an example of bartering. You agreed with each other the amount of products you wanted to swap, and then made the swap. In the past, people have traded many different things this way, including food, such as fruit and vegetables, or skills, such as sewing and shoe polishing, and even animals, such as goats and pigs. Say someone needed their shoes shining – they might have paid someone else two apples for the service. Or if a farmer needed new clothes for their family, they might have given the tailor a pig in exchange for all of their work. You may have bartered yourself without even knowing it. Have you ever made a deal with your parents to do a few chores around the house in exchange for something you really wanted? If so, clever bartering, my friend. **YOU'VE GOT THE RIGHT IDEA ALREADY.**

But the bartering system wasn't perfect. What would happen if you, as the town's apple seller, needed something, such as more baskets, or some milk, but it wasn't apple-picking season so you didn't have anything to barter with? You'd suddenly struggle to get anything you needed until the apples were ripe again. And what if you wanted to barter for something outside of your local community? Apples or pigs could be heavy or tricky to move over long distances.

MONEY, MONEY, MONEY

THE ULTIMATE GUIDE TO MONEY

This situation was a common problem, so people came up with a solution. They began to exchange objects such as metal, shells or gems for valuable items or skills. These same objects could then be used by people to trade for other items they needed. What a brilliant idea! This meant that even if it wasn't apple-picking season, you could still get the things you needed, as these objects were available all year round.

> Did you know Italians have used wheels of cheese as money since the Middle Ages and Fijians used the teeth of whales? (In fact, whale teeth are still an important part of Fijian culture to this day.) Pretty sharp thinking if you ask me.

From around 2,700 years ago, these objects started to be replaced by coins made from metal, including gold and silver. The shape and design of coins changed from place to place. Some looked like beans, others were round and had holes in the middle and some had faces on them – it was a great way for kings, queens and rulers to show off their faces long before newspapers and the internet.

MONEY, MONEY, MONEY

China invented the first paper money about 1,000 years ago, but the rest of the world didn't catch on to the idea until about 400 years ago. Whereas coins made of gold and silver were worth something because of the value of the metal, the notes acted more like an **'I OWE YOU'** – meaning that if you gave them to someone, you owed that person the amount of gold or silver coins listed on the banknote. It's like if you didn't have any pocket money left but you *really* wanted to buy a new comic, so you asked your older sibling to use their money to get it for you and you promised to pay them back later.

The money we have today has changed a lot since then. It's not just royalty, gods and presidents with their faces on coins and notes any more. **There are also famous writers, activists and scientists.** But how do the people in charge choose whose faces go on coins and notes? Well, it changes from country to country. In the USA, for example, you can't use the face of anyone living. Former president Abraham Lincoln appears on the $5 note and former president George Washington appears on the 25 cent coin.

And in South Africa in the 1990s, to mark a shift from the country's history of separating people by their race and discriminating against anyone who wasn't white, the country decided not to show any people at all. Instead, their money featured five animals – the rhinoceros, elephant, lion, Cape buffalo and leopard.

THE ULTIMATE GUIDE TO MONEY

Images found on money continue to change over time because **MONEY IS CONSTANTLY UPDATED**. In the UK, when King Charles III became king after his mother, Queen Elizabeth II, died in 2022, new coins and banknotes needed to be designed to show the new king. On one side, they have a portrait of King Charles III. (When you get your hands on one of the coins you'll notice that he's facing the left-hand side. But if you look at an old coin featuring Queen Elizabeth II, you'll notice she's facing to the right. This is because it's tradition for the new monarch to be facing the opposite direction to the monarch who came before them.) On the other side of the coin is an animal or flower to reflect the king's love for nature and wildlife. The animals include bees, a red squirrel and a puffin. The flowers are the national flower for each nation: a rose for England, a shamrock for Northern Ireland, a thistle for Scotland and a daffodil for Wales. The updated coins started being used in 2023.

SIR ISAAC NEWTON

One of the reasons money changes over time is to stop people from copying the designs and making and spending fake money that looks real. This is called **forgery**. It's a big problem and people who forge money can get into **A LOT OF TROUBLE**. Imagine if you made clothes and you spent time making a sick T-shirt. You then sell the finished merch to someone for £20, but when you try to use that £20 note elsewhere you find out it's fake so you can't spend it. In other words, it has no value. You'd be angry, right? Well, there was a lot of forged money going around at the end of the seventeenth and start of the eighteenth centuries. That's when Sir Isaac Newton came along to find a solution.

Now, you might have heard of **ISAAC NEWTON** – he was a *next-level* smart guy, especially at maths and science. He was the one who figured out how gravity works (that's the force that keeps us on the ground and stops us from floating off into space!). But there's one thing he's less well-known for and that is his work with money. You see, Isaac took a job at the Royal Mint – the company in the UK where the country's coins were made (and still are!). Back then, coins were made from gold and silver (today they're made from a mixture of metals).

But the gold and silver that was used to make the coins was often worth more than the value of the coins themselves! So it was no surprise that people would melt the coins down and sell the raw metal, even though it was illegal. It's like having a £2 coin but being able to get £3 if you melted the coin and sold the metal to someone. **WILD, RIGHT?** And to make things worse, people would also create fake coins from a mixture of metals, rather than just silver and gold. Basically, it was a big mess.

Isaac's job was to solve these problems...

...and a whole load more. So he did something drastic. He made everyone send all their money back to the Royal Mint, and he created entirely new coins with a whole new look. These coins were all a similar size and weight, had images on both sides, bumps round the edges and the metal used to make each coin had the same value as the coin itself. While it didn't completely get rid of forgery, making fake money was suddenly way more difficult because the coins were much harder to copy. **THANKS TO HIS INCREDIBLE WORK, THE ROYAL MINT IN LONDON BECAME THE MOST TRUSTED COIN MINT IN THE WORLD.**

Today the Royal Mint doesn't just make coins for the UK; they produce coins for more than sixty countries around the world! And they are always updating these coins to make them hard to forge. The pound coin, for example, used to be round, but the Royal Mint realized the design was being copied. So, in 2017 they released a new pound coin with twelve sides – along with lots of other new features.

The way that money has changed over time is fascinating, and the possibilities for the future are endless! In the last ten years or so, more and more businesses have stopped taking cash payments, and technology has developed so people can now pay for things using their smartphones and smartwatches. Perhaps we're heading for a future where society is completely cashless. But no matter how much money changes, one thing remains the same – it's an incredibly important part of our lives, and as with all important things, it's worth knowing the history behind it to truly understand it.

MONEY 101

Now, before we dive into the game and try to make that million, I want to give you some tips about how to look after your cash.

Think of these tips as the basics – the important things to keep in mind throughout the game, but also in real life.

As a financial advisor, people often come to me and ask me what they should do with their money. Now, as much as I would love to say, 'Pay for me to go on an all-expenses-paid holiday to Barbados,' that's not the kind of advice they're really looking for (sad, I know). My job is to give them advice on **HOW TO GROW THEIR MONEY**, make choices that will benefit their future and help them reach their goals, whatever they may be.

So before we get started on the game, I want to know what *your* goal is. Or maybe you have more than one. People often have a short-term goal – something they want to achieve quite quickly – and a long-term goal – something they hope to achieve in the future. Maybe your short-term goal is to buy a new games console or go on a trip to a theme park with your friends this summer. But you might also have long-term goals, such as going to university or saving for driving lessons when you're older. There's absolutely no wrong answer; after all, they are *your* goals. Take a moment to think about the things you want and write them down somewhere.

MONEY, MONEY, MONEY

In order to make your dreams a reality, you're probably going to need some money to help you get there.

That's why making smart choices with money is so important – it can help us achieve our goals and dreams, no matter how big or small or far off in the future they are.

And that's what money is all about. It's not about growing your money for the sake of just having lots and lots of it.

> **We should strive to earn money so we can reach our goals, improve our lives and help others too.**

My happiness is not decided by the amount of money that I have in my bank account; it's more about how I use that money to improve myself, my life and the world around me.

THE 50-40-10 RULE

So how can we make sensible decisions with money to help us achieve our goals? Well, let me tell you about my handy little guide called the **50-40-10 RULE**. You'll see that I come back to this rule quite a few times during the game. But rules are also there to be broken. So there are times when I suggest that we *don't* stick to the rule, and hopefully, as we make our way through the game, you'll understand why.

The 50-40-10 rule is a simple **budget**. A budget is basically a plan for your money. It tells you how much money you have, how much you need to spend on the essential things (such as **rent** for your home, bills for electricity, water and internet, and for food and travel), and how much is left over at the end. Writing down a budget is a great way to make sure you don't spend more money than you actually have.

Normally I tell people to use this rule on the money they have left over after they've paid for all the things they need. And if you don't have any bills to pay for, I suggest you use this rule for all of your money.

Let's imagine you have £100. Here's how you'd use the 50-40-10 rule:

MONEY, MONEY, MONEY

1. PAY YOURSELF
2. PAY SOMEONE ELSE
3. GIVE BACK

1. PAY YOURSELF 50 per cent of your money. (50 per cent means half. If you divide the amount of money you have by 2, you'll get the answer. The sum for 50 per cent of £100 is: £100 ÷ 2 = £50.) I don't just mean give yourself some money for no reason. 'Paying yourself' actually means *investing* in yourself. See it like giving half of your money to your future self. Now to do that, you've got to know your goals, which is why I just asked you to write them down. The idea of paying yourself is that you can use that £50 to help yourself achieve those goals.

For example, you could use it to develop a skill or passion you have. Let's say you're a singer in a band and you want to start playing live gigs in front of an audience. You could spend £50 on some singing lessons to help improve your skills. As you become better, so does your band, and people will be more likely to want to see you perform. Goal achieved!

Another way to pay yourself is by building your **savings**. Savings is the word for the money that you put to one side in a piggy bank or bank account to use in the future (see page 38). Savings are useful because when an opportunity comes up – like a trip or an event you want to go to – you will be able to use the money that you have saved to pay for it.

THE ULTIMATE GUIDE TO MONEY

Think about the different times you might be given some extra money – perhaps on your birthday or for doing chores around the house. If you save 50 per cent of those coins over time (and have a little patience), it'll all add up to a useful sum for when you really need or want it.

2. PAY SOMEONE ELSE 40 per cent of your money. (Working out 40 per cent is a bit trickier than 50 per cent. You need to divide the amount of money you have by 100, to find out what 1 per cent is. Then you need to multiply the answer by 40. So to work out 40 per cent of £100 the calculation is: £100 ÷ 100 (per cent) = £1. £1 x 40 (per cent) = £40. This means £40 is 40 per cent of £100.)

Paying someone else basically means paying someone 40 per cent of your cash in exchange for something you want. Now, I'm not talking about the things that we need in our everyday lives. I'm talking about the things that we just *want*. And who doesn't like treating themselves? From a fresh pair of trainers that you've had your eye on for ages to a trip to the cinema to see that new film everyone is talking about, spending money on something you want can feel irresistible.

You might be confused about why I call this 'paying someone else' when you're getting something in return for your money. Well, it's because ultimately you're giving your money to someone else for these things.

When you're treating yourself it's a good time to think about **immediate gratification** versus **delayed gratification**. Gratification is the feeling you get after doing something that makes you happy. Immediate gratification is the instant happy feeling you get when you buy an item you want as soon as you see it, such as when you're a bit peckish and buy some sweets. That yummy taste is immediate, but then it's over. Gone. However, *delayed* gratification is resisting the temptation to spend your money straight away so that you can achieve a greater, longer-lasting reward in the future.

Don't get me wrong, there's nothing wrong with **A TREAT NOW AND AGAIN** that brings you immediate gratification – it's important to treat yourself – but I always advise people to try to find a balance between the two. Spending your money on treats ALL the time means you won't have any cash left to use towards your goals or anything saved up for when you might need it in the future.

Using the 40 per cent rule can help you limit how much you're spending on treats, to make sure you have some left over. So if you're about to pay someone else for something you want, and you're close to your 40 per cent limit for the month, you can ask yourself:

> Do I really need another pair of kicks?
> And could I wait a month or two
> until I can watch the film at home,
> rather than spending money on a cinema ticket?

THE ULTIMATE GUIDE TO MONEY

3. GIVE BACK 10 per cent of your money. (If you use the same formula as we used to work out 40 per cent, you can find out what 10 per cent of your money is. In this case, £100 ÷ 100 (per cent) = £1. £1 x 10 (per cent) = £10, so 10 per cent of £100 is £10.) 10 per cent might feel like a lot of money to say goodbye to, but if you've followed the rule, then you've already had £90 for yourself! Plus, helping others can sometimes feel even better than treating yourself.

I, FOR ONE, LOVE TREATING MY MUM because she's done so much for me. It makes me so happy to see her face light up when I surprise her with a bunch of her favourite flowers. Treating loved ones is a great way to show them how much you appreciate the things they do for you.

Another way I give back is by donating money to charities that mean a lot to me. I know how lucky I am to have certain things and it's important to me to give what I can to help others. The feeling I get when I give back is priceless.

But one thing we need to make sure of is that we don't give more than we can afford.

If you aren't able to give 10 per cent of your cash then don't worry – helping others doesn't always need to cost money. You could donate your time or other things instead. For example, you could donate clothes that no longer fit you to charity. Or you could bake something and sell it to friends, family and neighbours, and give the money you make to a charity.

You can't help everyone, but you can always help someone.

You might be thinking, *Eman, I'm just a kid, I'll worry about all this when I'm older.* But honestly, these are great practices to get into now.

Take fourteen-year-old me. I would wash cars for my neighbours at weekends. I charged £5 per car and had four neighbours who were regular customers. Most weekends, I made £20 (£5 x 4 cars = £20) – that's £80 a month. At the end of each month I used all my cash, right down to the last penny, to buy either basketball trainers or video games for my PlayStation. I spent *all* of my money treating myself.

At the time I wasn't thinking about my future; my goal was impressing my friends at school and having fun. But now when I look back I realize it wasn't the smartest goal to have. There's nothing wrong with having fun, but I should have also thought about my long-term goals.

THE ULTIMATE GUIDE TO MONEY

What I could have done instead was split up my money with my 50-40-10 rule. From the £80 I earned each month, I would have had £40 to pay myself (£80 ÷ 100 (per cent) = £0.8. £0.8 x 50 (per cent) = £40), £32 to pay someone else (£80 ÷ 100 (per cent) = £0.8. £0.8 x 40 (per cent) = £32) and £8 to give back (£80 ÷ 100 (per cent) = £0.8. £0.8 x 10 (per cent) = £8).

By the way, there aren't exactly four weeks in a month – in fact, most months have four weeks and either one, two or three days. But to keep things simple, let's pretend there are.

Then, with my first month's earnings, I could have spent £10 of my **'PAY YOURSELF'** money to print a hundred flyers advertising my car-washing business and saved the rest. This would have helped me get more customers and, in turn, make more money. And then each month after that if I'd saved up all of my 'pay yourself' money, from the age of fourteen up until I got my first proper job when I was twenty-two, I would have had £3,840 (that's £40 a month saved for eight years! £40 x 12 months = £480 saved each year. £480 x 8 years = £3,840. £3,840 - £10 (flyer printing) = £3,830). That's a really nice number – and it's not even including the tips I would have made over the years, or the fact that my business would have grown. I probably would have been earning even more money each month!

And I still would have had £32 a month to spend on treating myself, meaning **I WOULD'VE ENJOYED THE BENEFITS OF MY HARD WORK** while also working towards my financial goals. Balance, remember? And I also could have given £8 a month to a charity or organization that I wanted to support.

> OK, thanks for sticking with me.

I know you're itching to **START THE GAME** and get on the road to **MAKING YOUR MILLION**! Hopefully now you understand the history of money and the basics of spending and saving it, you'll be able to stay on track to achieve your goals, not just in this game, but in life too. And don't worry, I'm not disappearing and leaving you to play solo. I'm going to play with you – giving you my tips and advice as we go, weighing up each option along the way.

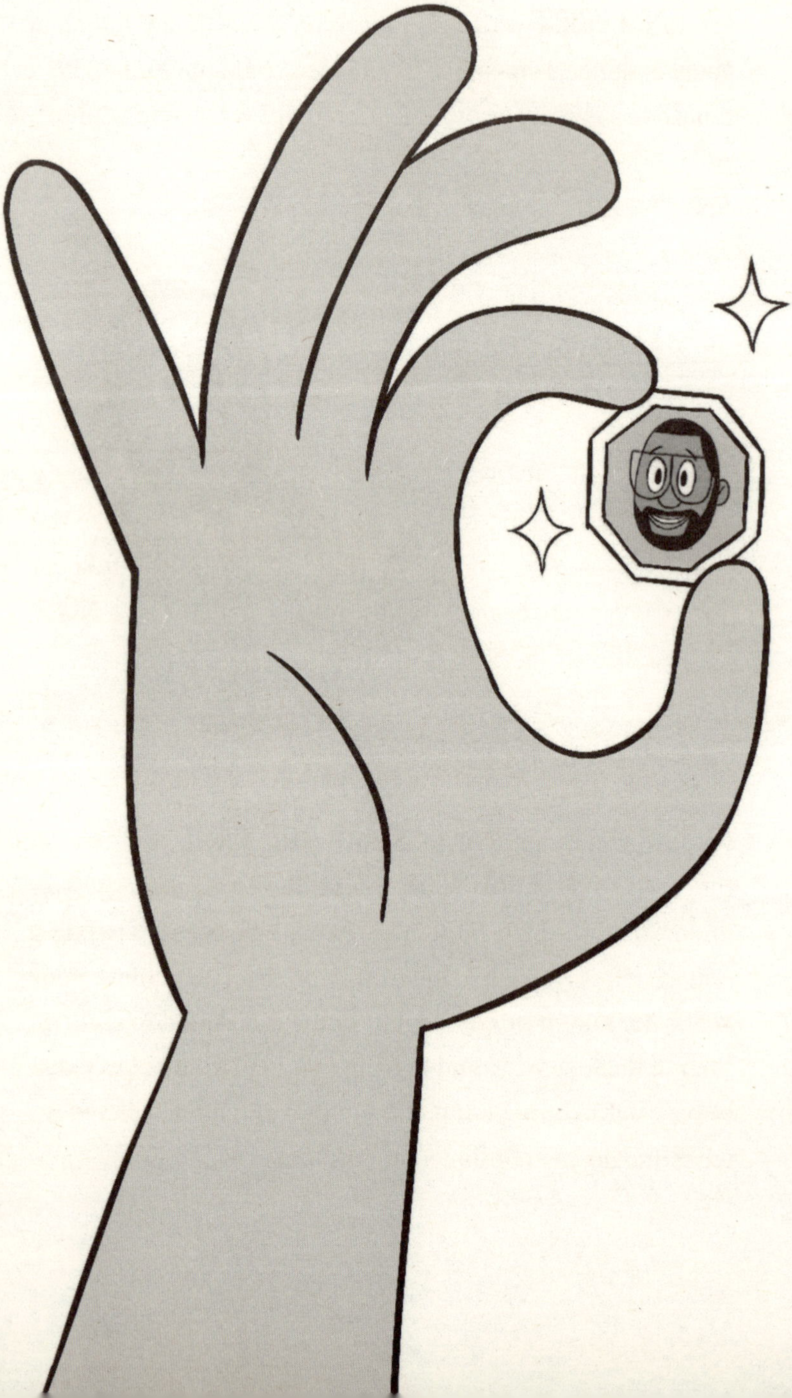

CHAPTER 2
LET THE GAMES BEGIN!

Are you ready to begin your journey to becoming a millionaire? Can you take a single coin and multiply it a million times? I bet you usually wouldn't put much thought into what you would do with a pound, but if you make the right choices here, you really could turn it into a million. And I don't mean pigs, apples, shells or gems – **I MEAN £1,000,000 OF MONEY**.

So here's how it's going to work. At the start of each chapter, I'll give you three options to choose from. There'll be lots of different paths you can take in this book, but there's never truly a right or wrong one. At the end of the day, only you know which choice is right for you. But if you want to go down the path to a million pounds, there are definitely some choices that will help you get there quicker than others.

Pick whichever option makes the most sense to you. And remember, your goal here is to try to make a nice million, so that's what you're working towards. If your goal was different, you might choose different options. But focus on the goal.

You might know which option you want to go with straight away or you might be hovering between a couple of choices, so my mates **ASH**, **CHEN** and **SAM** are going to give you their thoughts on the options. Finally, at the end of each chapter, there will be the big reveal – Eman's pick. This is the option I would choose, and it'll lead us on to the next chapter and closer to the goal of reaching a mill. If you pick something different to me, don't stress – it doesn't mean it's not a good shout. **After all, there's no exact formula for how to become a millionaire** (if there was one, we'd all be millionaires by now!). I'm just letting you know, with my financial advisor hat on, what I'd do. People all over the world have very different approaches to how they make their money. In fact, we'll meet some of these people throughout the game. And whether you're more of a cautious 'saver', a risk-taking 'investor' or a spontaneous 'spender', in real life you'll be able to make your own choices with your money. My hope is that this game will help guide you to making smart money decisions that are right for you.

One last thing before we start – we're going to stretch reality a bit in this game. That's because not all of the options you're going to choose from are things you could do in real life

LET THE GAMES BEGIN!

Chen

Ash

Sam

31

at your age. But they are all things you could do once you turn eighteen. So, we're going to practise being adults and have you trading on the **stock market**, buying houses and growing a business. Then, when it's time to do this stuff for real, you'll have already done the groundwork and gained the knowledge you will need! **NOW LET'S GET GOING!**

TIME TO GROW £1 INTO £100

So you've got a pound coin, a single shiny pound. Maybe you found it at the bottom of your coat pocket; maybe you saved it from some leftover birthday money; or perhaps you're the kind of person who likes to help your elderly neighbour carry their shopping and they gave you £1 as a thank you. Whichever way it has come into your possession, it's yours now and it's full of possibilities and opportunities. So, I'd like you to take your first step to growing that money, and your first goal is to get it to £100. It's a small step to your goal of a million, but it's still quite a lot of money. That's enough to buy you a pretty epic LEGO set, a scooter for doing tricks or perhaps a couple of theme park tickets with leftover change for snacks!

LET THE GAMES BEGIN!

YOUR THREE OPTIONS

First things first. What to do with that shiny pound coin . . .

OPTION ONE: You stock up on as much pick 'n' mix as 100 pennies can buy. I mean, it's a pound. You'll probably have another one soon, and maybe then you can think about growing it. But for now – sweets, please!

Ash

> How is this even a question? I don't need to see the other options to tell you I'd go to the newsagent and get as much pick 'n' mix as I could! Those sweets ain't gonna eat themselves! Pounds come and go, stop stressing it and enjoy yourself. YOLO (You Only Live Once)!

OPTION TWO: You save it. But you're a smart kid. No piggy banks here – it's the twenty-first century! A bank is offering a sweet little deal. If you set up a bank account with them, they'll give you £100 for nothing! That's right, free money. (You can't see me, but I'm dancing right now. Who doesn't love free money?!) Option two would put you ahead of the game, pocketing £101. Nice!

Chen

You know I love pick 'n' mix, Ash, but free money, man! I mean, how many sweets can you really buy for a pound? This is that immediate gratification Eman was on about. They'll be gone in minutes, and you'll have spent the money. Just think of what you could get with £101...

OPTION THREE: You set up your own business – car washing! You get yourself down to a pound store and buy yourself some sponges – they're going two for a pound! Then you raid the cleaning supplies in your house and 'borrow' the mop bucket and some washing-up liquid. You start knocking door-to-door, offering to wash people's cars for £10 a pop. Ten motors later and you're sitting pretty with £100 in your pocket.

Sam

I get you, Chen, free money is mad tempting. But remember what Eman said: think long-term! If you want to win this thing, you need to make big money. After the hundred, where you gonna go, huh? You need to start grafting!

LET'S JUST GET REAL FOR A SECOND.

You might be thinking, *Yeah, yeah, Eman, but I'm not really going to turn a pound into a mill, am I? I'm just a kid.* Well, you're wrong. **PLAIN AND SIMPLE.** But don't just take my word for it. Have you ever heard of a young man called Junior Natabou? Junior is from Benin in West Africa, and he became a millionaire at just seventeen. That's right, he was still a kid. And he did it all by starting his own business. Let me tell you how.

When Junior was fourteen he became interested in digital communication, which means sending and receiving information electronically. Reading websites, sending text messages and posting or watching social media content – this is all digital communication. Junior decided to do some research about the industry and how it works. After watching a load of YouTube videos, he started something called a media-buying business. These businesses help companies decide where and when to **advertise** their products on television, radio and social media. They then help them buy those advertising slots.

Unfortunately, he made some mistakes and this business was unsuccessful. This is pretty normal – you wouldn't believe how many successful business people failed on their first attempt. But Junior learned a lot from this and his failure didn't stop him. He went on to open his own e-commerce business, which is a service that helps people buy and sell goods and services on the internet.

By the time he was seventeen, his business had made millions! Junior's story is a great reminder to us all that mistakes and failures shouldn't stop us from taking risks and **CHASING OUR DREAMS**, no matter what age we are.

Mistakes teach us lessons – lessons that can lead to amazing achievements!

LET THE GAMES BEGIN!

EMAN'S ADVICE

Feeling inspired? Right, let's get back to it. Chen, Sam and Ash all make some bangin' points. But I'm your finance man, and I'm here to help you understand the whys of these options. So let's drill down and get into the specifics.

OPTION ONE

Buying sweets. Sure, I get that, who doesn't like sweets?! And it's only £1; you could get another one easily enough, right? I reckon if you look down the back of your sofa or rifle through your parents' car you'll probably be able to double your money. But so what? The thing is, as we've seen, money is important – it's precious. It might be easy to think, *I'll just spend this £1 because more will come my way*, and while that may sometimes be true, it's not always a good attitude to have. Stuff might not always come your way, so it's important to value what you've got. So, sorry if you went for pick 'n' mix, but it ain't my pick.

OPTION TWO

Now, I like this one. Opening a bank account is a great thing to do and even sweeter if you can get some free money for doing it. I'm a big fan of free money – who isn't?! And £100 is a lot of free money. For some people, that's what they would make after working for a whole day!

But in this case, all you'd need to do is open a bank account.

You might be thinking, *Hold up, Eman, why are the bank giving me free bills? That doesn't make sense.* So let's discuss bank accounts. A bank is a business that borrows and saves money. Every customer of a bank has an account, which is like a file that records how much money that person has saved with, or borrowed from, that bank, and how much they have spent from their own account. **EASY ENOUGH.**

You may already have a bank account, and if not, people aged under sixteen can open one with a parent or guardian. There are two main types of bank accounts: a **current account** and a **savings account**. A current account is where people tend to keep money for the things they pay for regularly, such as bus or train tickets, food, clothes, going out with mates and hobbies. Think of 'current' as meaning 'now' – in other words, it holds the money you want to use immediately and easily.

LET THE GAMES BEGIN!

A savings account is for anything you *don't* plan to buy very often. So it's where people keep their money that they are saving to use in the future. Savings accounts pay **interest**, which is a percentage of money given to customers as a reward for choosing to save their money with that bank.

SAY YOU PUT £100 IN A SAVINGS ACCOUNTS AND THE BANK OFFERS 1.5 PER CENT INTEREST EACH YEAR.

At the end of the first year, they would give you £1.50 for saving that money with them (to work out 1.5 per cent of £100 the calculation is: £100 ÷ 100 (per cent) = £1. £1 x 1.5 (per cent) = £1.50. This means £1.50 is 1.5 per cent of £100).
WIN!

Savings accounts keep our money in a safe place and help us resist the temptation of spending it all at once. The longer you keep your money in a savings account, the more interest you will make on your money. Delayed gratification, remember?

You might be thinking, *But why do I need a bank account at all? Can't I just keep my money in a drawer or under the bed?* I mean, you could, but I wouldn't recommend it.

Firstly, a bank account is much safer. If it's just under the bed, someone could break in and take it when you were out, and there'd be no way to get it back.

Secondly, you wouldn't be able to use it when you were out and about. Imagine you go out and don't take any money with you because you hadn't planned on buying anything, but then you see something you really like. You'd have to go all the way back home, go under the bed, get your money and then head back out to buy it. By the time you get back to the store the thing you wanted might have gone and you'd miss out! Plus lots of places don't even take cash any more.

You also can't pay for Netflix or buy anything online with cash from under your bed. And when you're older, companies normally pay **wages** into a bank account, and it's through this account that you'll also pay for bills, rent and other important things.

If you have a bank account, as long as you have a bank card or a banking app on your phone, you can pay for anything anywhere, and receive money easily too.

But while all of this is good life advice, it doesn't set us up to earn more. Focus on that million pound goal, remember! Option two is a quick and easy way to get an extra £100 - but where are you going from there? What's the plan? You need a plan to keep you focused on reaching your long-term goal.

LET THE GAMES BEGIN!

I need to be straight with you for a second. In the real world, free money for opening up a bank account is typically only offered to people over eighteen. But there are still perks to setting one up before then – some banks offer a free piggy bank or higher interest rates when you open an account. So if you're planning on opening a bank account, ask a parent or guardian to help you do the research to make sure you get the best deal possible.

OPTION THREE

I think this is a sound choice. Obviously I'm going to say that – washing cars is what I did when I was young to make some extra money.

> But what I really like is the potential.

You're not just setting yourself up to reach £100, you're thinking beyond that. This option has got a lot of positives. But as with all things, you have to take time to weigh up the pros (the benefits) and the cons (the negatives or costs).

And the biggest cost here is going to be your time. Time is so, so important! In fact, it's probably the most important thing you have, alongside your health, and WAYYYY more important than money.

Money without time is worthless.

If you stop and think about it, why do we want to make money? To pay our bills and have some left over to enjoy our time better! So you need to make sure you spend your time wisely.

Back to washing cars – is it a good use of time? I reckon so. If you balance things well, get your homework done during the week and get up early and wash cars on Saturday mornings, then you'll be free for the rest of the weekend to live life. I'd say that's time pretty well spent.

For me – what would I do? Well, I like the look of option two and option three. But the way I see it is, sure, option two takes a lot less work – it's free money and who doesn't love that? – yet at the end of the day, it's having a business that will help you reach the ultimate million-pound goal.

You might be asking why you couldn't just take the free money and then start a business (and I like your thinking). But whether you start a business now, or after opening a bank account, free money ain't enough. You need ideas.

LET THE GAMES BEGIN!

EMAN'S PICK

So my pick is option three! It's a good use of your time – and you know how important I think time is – and helps us step closer to our goal quicker. But if you picked something else, don't worry. This is a game; we're just playing here. Hopefully you understand my reasons for choosing option three (or a combination of options two and three), and remember we're here to make mistakes, practise, live and learn, so when it comes to the real stuff we can use our new knowledge and experience to make good choices.

So there you have it, that's my take! What are you thinking? Have you got a sweet tooth, so you're heading to the newsagent with Ash? Or are you focusing on making gains? Whichever option you choose, remember there's no right or wrong one. It's your money and you know your needs best. So if you strongly believe in one option, then go for it. You do you.

And just like that (well, with some wise choices and a few buckets of soapy water) you've turned £1 into £100.

STARTING A BUSINESS

Before we move on to turning that hundred into a crisp grand (a 'grand' is another word for £1,000), I want to talk to you a little bit about starting a business or a side hustle. Business is all about creating something that adds value to people and their lives.

When it comes to setting up a business, people usually struggle with where to start. I get it. It can feel pretty overwhelming starting a business from scratch! So the best place to begin is with something that comes easily to you. And when I say easy, I mean something you either enjoy doing or something you already do – that way it won't feel too challenging.

If Cas down the road has a nice little side hustle designing websites for people, that's great. But if you can't even work out how to upload a video to TikTok, is a side hustle in tech really a smart option for you? Rather than trying to copy what other people are doing, think about what *you* can already do really well or what you find yourself doing often.

I always say, '**KEEP IT SIMPLE**'. Your first business shouldn't require loads of money or years of training. Me, I like cars, so washing cars was a simple option that I knew I'd enjoy. What do you like?

What do you do for fun? What are the hobbies or activities you do all the time that you could make some money (or 'dough') off?

We all have *something* we're good at (even if it's not immediately obvious) – cleaning, drawing, singing, writing, sports, anything! There will always be someone out there who can benefit from your skills.

Are you good at looking after your own pets? Maybe offer a pet-feeding service for small animals such as cats, rabbits, guinea pigs and hamsters for when your neighbours go away on holiday. (It's a good idea to ask a parent or guardian to come with you the first couple of times and to be in charge of locking up.) Got some serious coding skills? Offer to tutor people and share your knowledge. Got more energy than you know what to do with? Use it to help people who move at a slower pace – maybe cut their grass, get rid of weeds or shift anything heavy they can't manage. Like I said earlier, one of the main reasons why we make money is to enjoy our time better. That's the real value of money. So if we can enjoy ourselves while making it, then the better and happier we will feel.

And remember, you will have wins, but you will also make mistakes along the way, just like Junior Natabou. Everyone does. But with the right attitude, this experience will develop you into a skilled, knowledgeable and confident business owner.

Once you've got your business idea – whether it's pet-sitting, doing chores, car washing, cleaning or anything else suited to your skills – you need to figure out who would pay money for your product or service and how you are going to attract them to it. In the business world, this is called a **target market**.

THINK ABOUT IT: there's no point advertising your car-washing business to your friends because they don't have cars. But their parents might – so there's your target market. Or maybe you love to bake cakes and want to turn this into a business. This time your friends could be a good shout, they might buy a cupcake or two, but to make bigger bucks you probably want to widen your target market. You could try their parents again or see if any local sports clubs want to buy some cakes to give out to their teams as a post-match celebration. (Though just remember, we're living in Eman's fantasy finance world here. In real life, you'll need things like special insurance for car washing, and food-hygiene certificates for anything that involves preparing food to be sold.)

LET THE GAMES BEGIN!

Once you've got your target market, you'll need to advertise. This is how you let people know about the product or service you're selling. 'Word-of-mouth' is a great – and free! – option. It basically means you provide your service to people who then tell the people they know how good your business is.

Then those people (hopefully) become your customers too and continue to spread the word.

Alternatively, you could print leaflets to advertise your business. Maybe give them to your friends to pass on to their parents. Or politely ask to leave them in places such as on a local noticeboard, in a community centre or in a shop window.

FINALLY, before we get back to the serious business of making our million, we need to talk about **profit**. The aim of a business is pretty much always to make a profit. And profit is going to help you reach your goal. Profit is when you sell something for more than what it cost you. For example, if you spend £2 on the ingredients for some cupcakes and sell them for £6, you'll have made £4 profit (£6 (price) - £2 (ingredients) = £4 (profit)). But there's something missing from this equation.

Can you think what it is?

THE PRICE OF YOUR TIME! This is *really* important because your time is valuable. I wouldn't keep saying it if it wasn't true! If you're going to put the time in, make sure you pay yourself! Let's go back to the cupcakes.

Say you want to be paid £5 for every hour you work. If it takes you two hours to bake, prepare and then sell twelve cupcakes, that means it'll cost you £12 in total to make the cupcakes (£10 for your time (£5 x 2 hours) + £2 for the ingredients).

And this can be how you decide how much to sell your cupcakes for. You want to make sure that you sell your cupcakes for more than £12 to make a profit. So if it was me, I'd sell these cupcakes for £1.50 each. Once you've sold all twelve cupcakes, you'll have made £18 (12 x £1.50 = £18). This means that you'll have made £6 profit (£18 (money from customers) - £2 (ingredients) - £10 (wages) = £6 (profit)).

GETTING THE PRICE RIGHT IS VERY IMPORTANT. You don't want to price items or services too low and not make enough money to pay yourself or make a profit, because then it wouldn't be worth all that effort you put in. But also, if the shop down the road is selling similar cupcakes for 75p each and you price yours at £1.50 each, people will probably buy their cupcakes from the shop because they're half the price.

LET THE GAMES BEGIN!

So you have to look at what similar businesses are charging. Could you price your offering a little bit cheaper to make it more appealing (while still making a profit)? Or could you price it a bit higher but make this worthwhile for customers by adding extra things that your competitors don't have? For example, you could offer free bespoke icing options. Or if you have a tutoring business, you could offer an extra ten minutes' free tutoring if people sign up for three sessions. Prices can make or break a business, so it's important to get it right.

So, how much could you charge for your business idea? What's that? Oh, you need a moment to compare prices with those of your competitors? Smart move! Take as much time as you need. **I'LL BE WAITING!**

And there you have it: a super-quick intro to business. Hopefully these tips will be helpful starting points for your brand-new side hustle.

Now it's time to get back to the business of this book – making a mill!

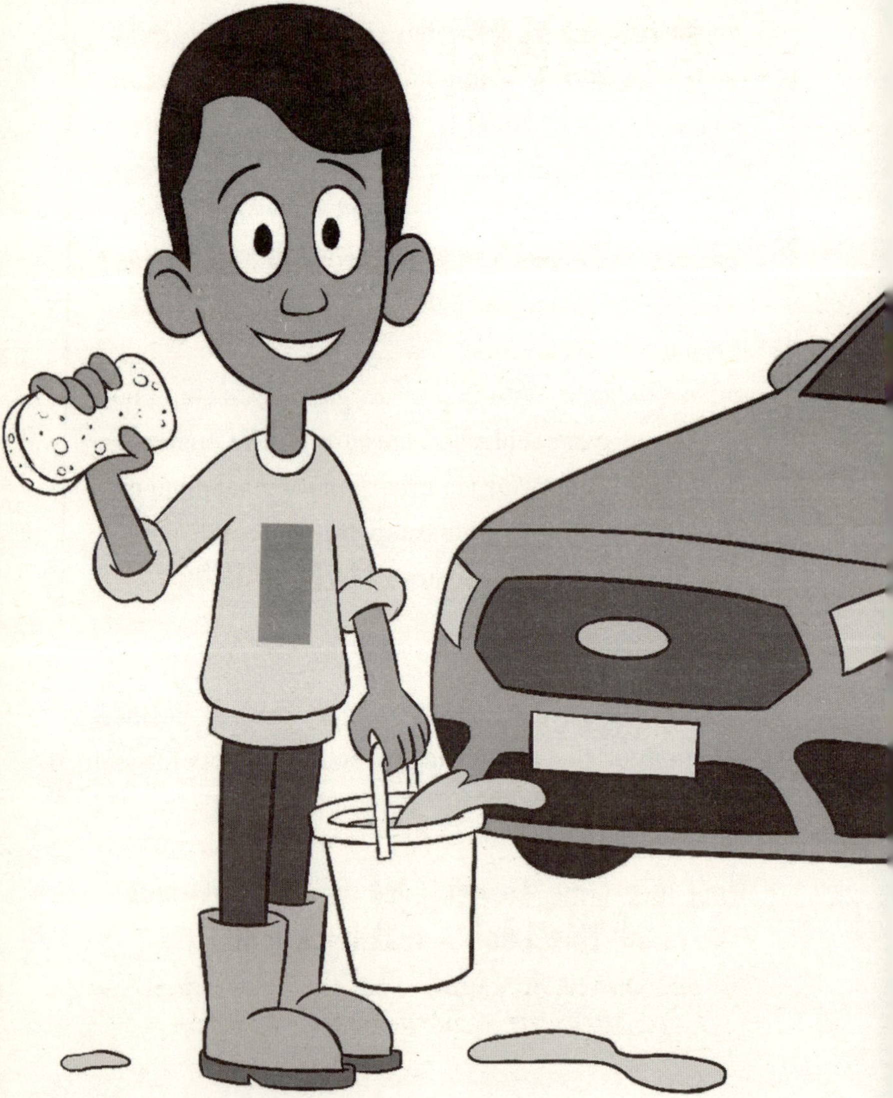

CHAPTER 3
TIME TO MAKE A GRAND

Job one, done – you turned £1 into £100. Serious respect. And this time we're looking to go a step further and add another zero, turning that £100 into £1,000! Making a grand is a big task. With that much money you could buy not one but two games consoles, the latest top-of-the-range iPhone, a season ticket for your favourite football club and entrance to that music gig you're desperate to go to! It's a lot of money. But it's OK, I'm here along with Ash, Sam and Chen to guide you through it. Are you ready?

KLAXON ALERT

IT'S YOUR BIRTHDAY!
A FAMILY MEMBER IS SPREADING THE LOVE AND FEELING EXTRA GENEROUS, AND THEY'VE GIVEN YOU £100 AS A GIFT – NICE ONE! YOU'VE DOUBLED YOUR MONEY AND YOU DIDN'T EVEN HAVE TO DO ANYTHING. (DON'T MIND ME, I'M JUST OVER HERE DOING MY FREE MONEY DANCE AGAIN!)

TURN £100 INTO £1,000

Life is full of ups and downs, and people choosing to share their hard-earned money with you is definitely an up. So, let's appreciate that, and say a massive 'thank you'. Now that you've got £200 in the bank, you're that little bit closer to your goal. Just another £800 to go, so let's look at our options to grow that money.

YOUR THREE OPTIONS

OPTION ONE: Expansion, baby! Let's get rich quick. You've done some research and realized that growing your business is key. At the moment, you wash ten cars a week near your house all by yourself, but if you invite some people to join your business who can start washing cars at different locations outside your local area, you'll be able to make more money. It'll cost a bit to set up – extra supplies and hiring people to help won't come for free. So, you'll need to take out a £1,000 **loan** to cover the extra costs of supplies and people's wages. If you use this loan to open nine more car-washing sites, you could hit the goal sharpish. You normally make £100 a week with one car wash, but with ten sites, it'd only take you two weeks to earn £2,000 (10 (sites) x £100 = £1,000. £1,000 x 2 (weeks) = £2,000) – that's enough to pay back the loan and hit that £1,000 target.

TIME TO MAKE A GRAND

> *This is a no-brainer! I don't need to hear any more. Option one, baby! You should expand the business and make more money! You've seen how it can work with just one site; imagine the money you can make with ten! It would be a lot of work, but the reward would be greater. Nothing great has been achieved without work, right? Put the work in, grow your business and you'll make that million in no time!*

Sam

OPTION TWO: Take your car-washing hustle to a new level and offer more services to your loyal customers! Rather than just doing a standard car clean, you've realized that some of your customers would like their cars waxed too, to keep them cleaner for longer and extra shiny. On the advice of one of your regular customers, you visit a **wholesalers** and make the most of their bulk-buy offers. (Don't worry, I'll explain all these terms in a minute.) Using your £200, you buy a sturdy bucket, new sponges, polishing cloths, car shampoo, five tubs of car wax and – get this – *fifty* phone cases! Why phone cases? Well, it means you can add *another* product to your growing business. All in, you spend £195. You're still doing ten car washes a week, but you also convince half of your customers to get their cars waxed for an extra tenner a pop.

THE ULTIMATE GUIDE TO MONEY

In addition, you sell ten phone cases a week for £10 each – you're also adding extra value to your product by personalizing them with people's initials using an old stencil and some paint you found in your room. You're making £250 a week and, in just four weeks, you'll have reached the £1,000 target. (£100 a week for washing cars + £50 a week for waxing cars + £100 a week for selling phone cases = £250. £250 x 4 weeks = £1,000)

Chen

I get where you're at with option one, Sam – sometimes you need to spend money to make money. But taking out a loan seems like risky business – right, Eman? I'd check out the wholesalers thing in option two instead.

OPTION THREE: Keep doing what you're doing, plugging away at your car-washing business. You're turning over £100 a week and your customers are loyal, so you decide not to change anything. In just eight weeks, with your earnings and the £200 already in your pocket, you'll hit that £1,000 (£100 a week for washing cars x 8 weeks = £800. £800 + £200 = £1,000).

TIME TO MAKE A GRAND

> *You're having a laugh, Sam, even more locations?! Sure, you'd make a nice profit, but ten businesses to manage sounds like A LOT of work to me! Washing cars ain't easy, never mind managing ten sites. Plus, I don't know about you, but it'd eat into my gaming time. You're already making money and you'll still hit Eman's goal, eventually. Why mess with a good thing? I'd take option three so you can still make money and have some free time.*

Ash

EMAN'S ADVICE

There are some good options here, and one way or another they'd all get us to our goal, but let's look at each choice in a bit more detail.

OPTION ONE

Big respect for the ambition here. And growth is really important for a business, especially when you've got plans as big as ours, so I can understand the thinking. You've done it once, why not do it nine more times? It sounds easy. You could hire friends to manage the other sites and if it works, you'll be laughing all the way to the bank.

But what if one friend doesn't show up for work? What if you don't get enough customers at all ten locations each week? And what if you don't make enough to pay back that loan? That's a lot of 'ifs'.

CHEN IS RIGHT. Not being able to afford to pay back a loan is serious business. So let's stop for a second and get our heads around loans. A loan is an amount of money that customers borrow, often from a bank, and agree to pay back at a later date. Just like if you were to borrow some money from a sibling and promise to pay them back later. But the difference between borrowing from a sibling and borrowing from a bank is that with a bank you don't get the money for free – you usually have to pay interest on loans. Remember how we talked about what happens if you save money with a bank? They *pay* you interest for saving with them. (Head back to page 39 for a reminder.) Well, interest on loans works the other way around. Banks that give you loans normally *charge* you interest for borrowing money. And the interest charged for borrowing money is much higher than the interest you get for saving money.

What I mean is, if you save £1,000 with a bank, you might receive 1 per cent interest each year on your savings, which would be £10 (£1,000 ÷ 100 (per cent) = £10. £10 x 1 (per cent) = £10). But, if you take a loan of £1,000 from a bank, you might be charged 5 per cent interest on the money you

TIME TO MAKE A GRAND

borrow, which would be £50 (£1,000 ÷ 100 (per cent) = £10. £10 x 5 (per cent) = £50). So it costs a lot to borrow money, but you don't get anywhere near the same reward for saving it.

Now back to my question – what if you don't make enough money to pay back a loan? Well, the bank will keep adding interest over time, and potentially charge you with an extra fine for late payment as well. This means that the amount of money you have to pay back will just keep increasing until the debt is repaid. And if after a while you still can't pay the money back, the bank will come to take items that belong to you. The value of these items will add up to the amount you borrowed (plus the interest and fines). This is known as **repossession**. So, say you didn't pay back the £1,000 loan and you ended up owing the bank £1,500 because of the interest and fines added on. People who work as bailiffs (individuals employed by repossession companies) could come to your house and take things such as your Xbox, clothes, laptop and TV until they had gathered enough items to add up to a value of £1,500. It can be scary stuff.

With option one, it won't just be the £1,000 that you'll have to pay back. It will also be the interest. So even if everything were to run smoothly, it'd take you longer than two weeks to pay back the loan because you'd need to pay the interest too.

Taking out a loan *can* be a great option for a new business. But if it's not managed sensibly it can have very serious consequences, so you really need to look at the risks.

The risks with this option aren't all to do with the loan though. Growing a business quickly is also a risk. Ten car-washing sites is a lot and managing them all might take up more of your time than you expected. This could mean you fall behind on your schoolwork or you suddenly don't have enough time to hang out with friends or do after-school clubs. Remember how I said that part of the reason why we make money is to *enjoy* our time better? Well, I'd be worried this option doesn't leave a lot of room for enjoyment.

ISLAMIC FINANCE

Now, with all this talk of interest, you might be thinking that it's unfair for banks, people and companies to make more money from the money they already have! And you're not alone in thinking this way. Many Muslims follow the practices of Islamic finance, which means that the way they make money follows their religious teachings and beliefs. Islamic finance products and services aren't just for Muslims though. Anyone can use them.

TIME TO MAKE A GRAND

Islamic finance is based around the belief that money shouldn't have value by itself. Instead, it's just a way to buy and sell products and services that do have value, such as houses, food or books. This means that anyone who follows the rules of Islamic finance avoids paying or receiving interest. Why? Because with interest, someone makes money *from money*. Whether that's banks earning interest from a loan, or you earning interest from saving money with a bank, this goes against the Islamic view that money doesn't have value by itself.

So, if you agree with the ideas of Islamic finance and you are concerned that the options in this game don't align with your beliefs, please don't worry! There are Islamic finance alternatives to many of the options in this book, including Islamic finance **ISAs**, loans, **credit cards** and **mortgages** (and I'll explain all these terms later).

OPTION TWO

I rate the thinking here. Adding extra services to your business is a great way to grow it. While your customers wait for their car to be washed (and waxed), it is the perfect time for them to take a look at the phone cases you're selling. Hopefully your customers will be so impressed they'll tell other people about your business, using word-of-mouth to spread the news. Before you know it you could have more customers and be making even more money.

Adding different services or products to your business is a really **SMART THING TO DO** – loads of big companies do it. Take the company Uber, for example. Uber started out as a taxi company that offered people the ability to order a taxi from an app on their phone whenever they needed one. In the USA, before everyone had to go into lockdown and stay in their houses because of the Covid-19 pandemic, Uber had a similar number of customers as another taxi company called Lyft. But then people stopped taking taxis because they weren't able to go anywhere. So Uber decided to use all of their drivers in a different way. Rather than driving *people* around, they expanded their business to deliver food instead. They called it Uber Eats. Because of this extra service, Uber grew to have way more customers than Lyft. It's a great example of how adding something extra to your business can make a big difference.

But let's not forget how smart that customer of yours was for suggesting you go to a wholesaler. Why? Because wholesalers are companies that sell products in large quantities, or 'bulk'. Usually when you buy lots of the same item at the same time it lowers the cost per item. It's called an **economy of scale**. It might sound confusing, but it's actually quite simple! The more of a product you buy, the

TIME TO MAKE A GRAND

cheaper it becomes. Wholesalers can afford to do this because they buy their goods directly from the people or companies who make them in very large quantities. This is because it's cheaper for the wholesalers to sell in bulk, as they pay less for packaging and **distribution**.

It's great for businesses who need large quantities of the same product. Look at it this way. Your local shop gets a lower price on products because they buy hundreds of them from a wholesaler. But a supermarket would get an even lower price because they can afford to buy *thousands* of the same products from the wholesaler, as they have stores all over the country. So, buying sponges, clothes, phone cases and car wax in bulk, rather than individually, makes good business sense.

But you've got to be careful – don't get ahead of yourself and buy more phone cases than you can sell. It's no good if you've got a bedroom full of stuff no one wants. And remember to factor in your time! Personalizing those cases and waxing cars is all going to take a bit more time. You need to weigh up whether you think the money you will make is worth all the extra time and work.

OPTION THREE

I like it! You recognize you've got a good thing going and if you keep things as they are you won't put too much pressure on yourself or your time – which is always an important thing to consider.

But even though you'll hit that £1,000 eventually, if you don't grow your business and find a way to make more money, more quickly, then it's going to take you a loooooooong time to reach the goal of a million pounds. In fact, if you earned the same amount of money each week, and it never increased, it'd take you nearly 200 years to get there! So yeah, maybe it's not the *best* business plan for our goal . . .

SPOTIFY

One of the reasons I really like option one is the ambition. And that's a good thing. But being too ambitious too quickly can be harmful for even the biggest businesses.

At the start of 2023, Swedish company Spotify had to admit they'd made this very mistake. Spotify is a service through which users can listen to (or 'stream') millions of songs, podcasts and videos without having to buy them. During the Covid-19 pandemic everyone

TIME TO MAKE A GRAND

had to spend a lot of time at home, and this meant they were using online and streaming services, such as Spotify, more often than before. The online and streaming companies got excited by all this extra business, so they employed more people and offered extra services, such as lots more podcasts for users to listen to.

But the problem was, once people were able to leave their houses again, they stopped using these services as much. This left the businesses **SPENDING MORE MONEY THAN THEY WERE MAKING**, which is never good news. These companies had to admit to their mistakes and find ways to reduce costs so that they could start making more money again. In the case of Spotify, it meant 1,500 people lost their jobs. Amazon and Meta (the company that owns Facebook and Instagram) also made the same error and had to cut costs back down again after lockdown was over.

So, if your business starts to take off, just remember to think carefully about how quickly you want to grow. It's always safer to take your time and make careful decisions than to move too fast.

EMAN'S PICK

So, crunch time. Have you picked an option? Where do you think we should go from here?

This one is tough – all the options have some serious pros and cons, but to me there's a clear option to keep us on the path to a million, and that's option two – expanding your business with extra services.

It's a great way to increase how much money you're making each month and work towards the overall goal, without taking too much risk. It also won't take up *all* of your time, so you can still enjoy yourself on the weekends.

Selling extra things to my customers is something I wish I'd done when I was younger with my own car-washing business. Well, I wouldn't have sold phone cases because not everyone had mobile phones when I was your age. But maybe I could have sold nodding dogs. They were these little plastic dogs that looked out of the back window of your car and nodded as your drove along. They were all the rage when I was a kid. Ah well, you live and you learn, as they say. And I did learn, which is why I'm passing this lesson on to you.

That hard work and creativity have paid off. You've now got £1,000! You're storming ahead.

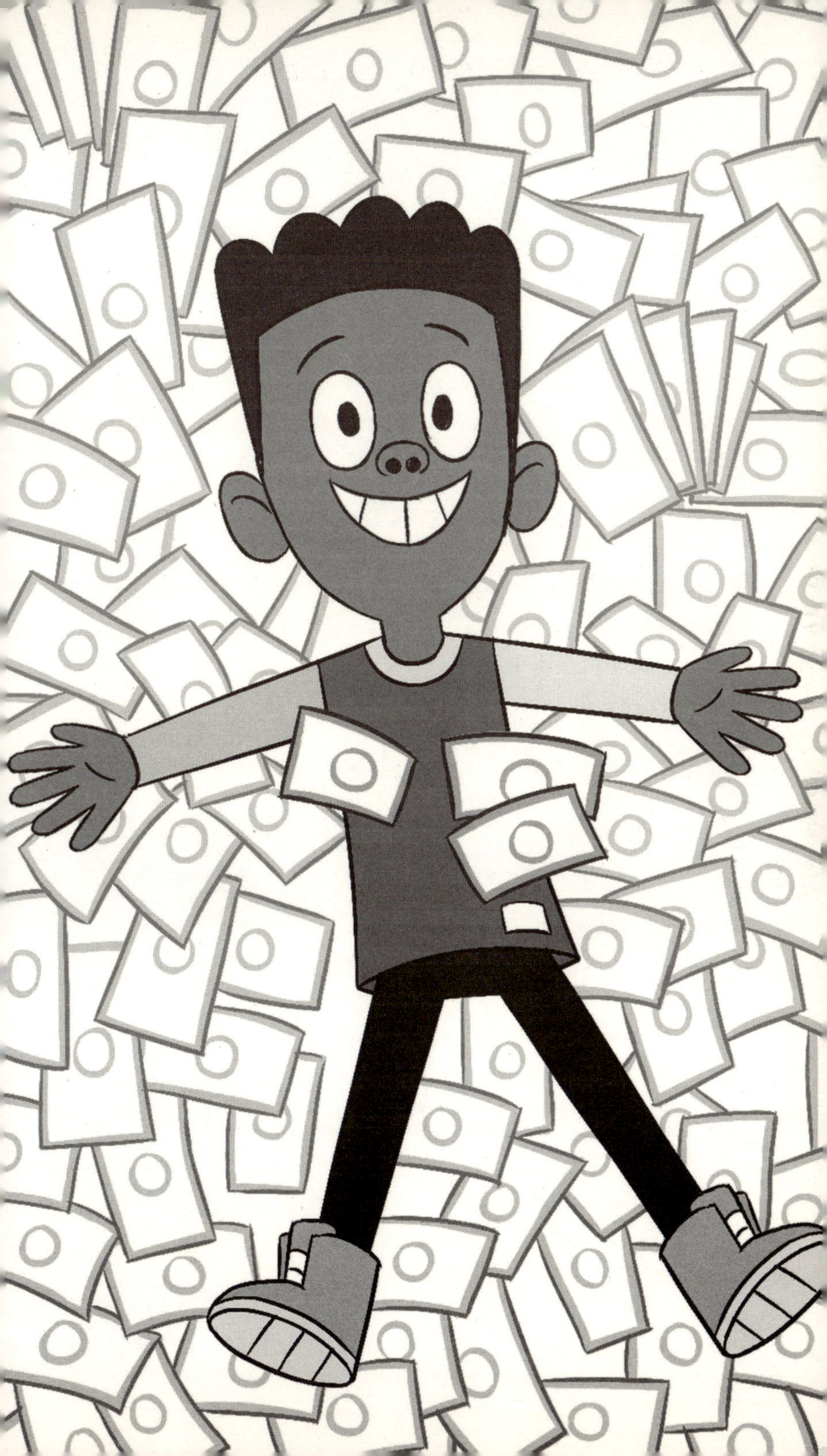

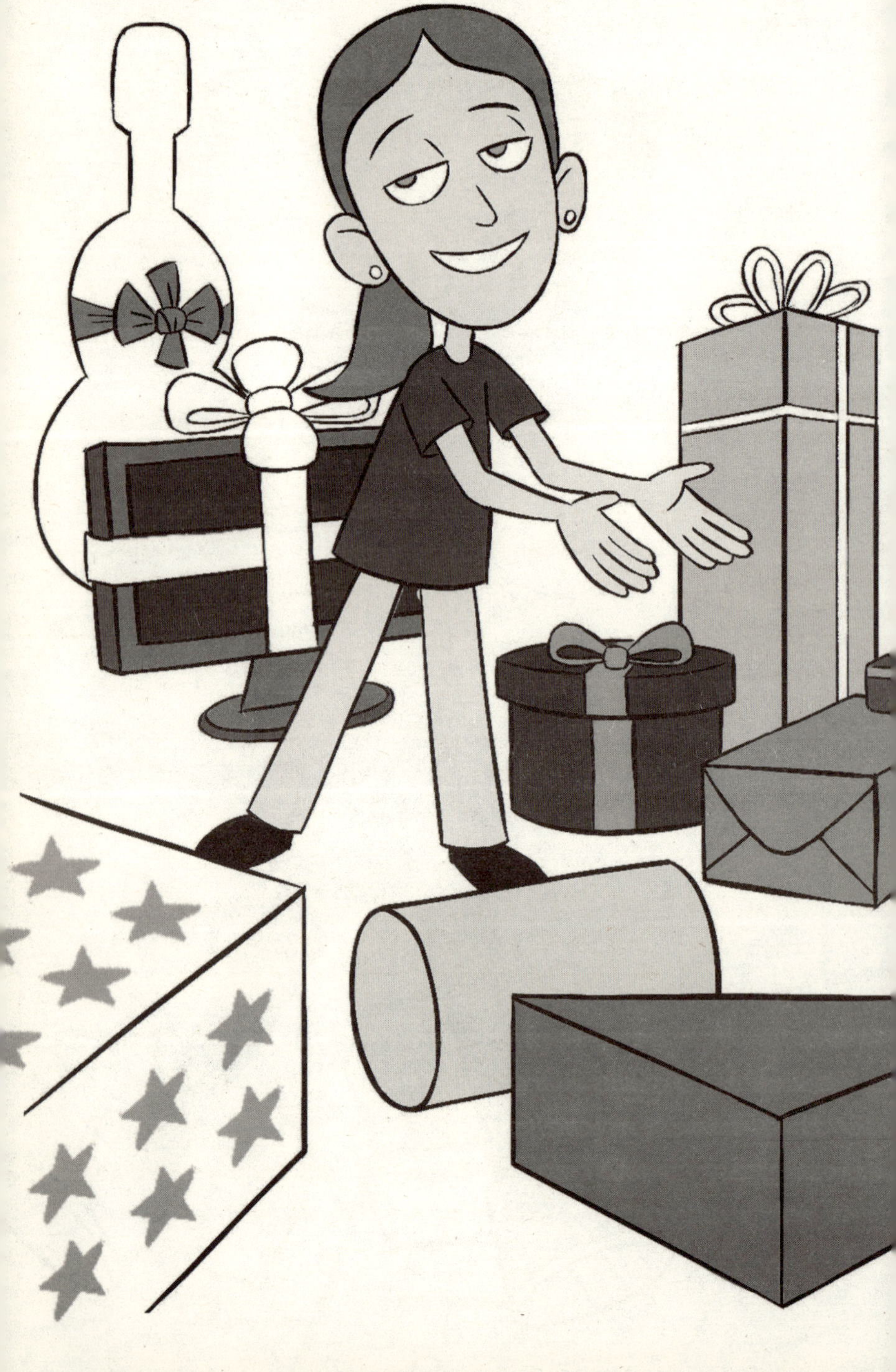

CHAPTER 4
STUNT OR SAVE

We're making serious gains here, people – shout out to you. You've gone from just one pound to a thousand of them. It's taken some smart thinking, sacrifices, self-control (believe me, I know how tempting it is to go and buy ALL the pick 'n' mix you can get your hands on) and hard work, but hopefully you can see that it's starting to pay off. We've still got a long, long way to go though, so don't lose focus just yet. Our next target is £5k (the 'k' just means thousand – so £5k is £5,000!). And £5,000 is A LOT of money. It could buy you 20,000 Freddo chocolate frogs (and make you feel very sick!) or a nice second-hand car!

GROW £1,000 TO £5,000

Before we dream about how we'd spend that money, we need to make it! So let's look at how things are going since we grew the business. Your car-washing business has been steadily gaining more customers. Also, just as we thought, word has spread about your cool phone cases and loads of people have been coming to you for your personalized goods. Adding extra products to sell in your business was a boss move! You're now earning £250 a week! That's an amazing achievement, but if you want to reach that million, you can't get too comfortable just yet. We're starting to get into some serious money here.

And for serious money we need serious ideas.

So pull out your business hat (mine is a navy-blue baseball cap, what's yours?) and let's look at ways we can turn £1,000 into £5,000.

YOUR THREE OPTIONS

OPTION ONE: Between schoolwork, hanging with your mates, clubs, chores, washing and waxing cars, and personalizing phone cases you're keeping **REAAAAL** busy. I'm tired just thinking about it! You really don't feel you have any extra time at the minute, so you're going to keep running the business as it is instead of expanding further. And you set up a current account to put your weekly earnings from the car washing into (see page 38). If you save every penny you make, £1,000 each month, then in five months you will have saved £5,000. Sure, it'll take time, but you're young. You have plenty of time! If you keep things up, you'll have saved up £120,000 in ten years!

STUNT OR SAVE

Sam

You know me, I'm normally all about the hard work. But I've got to admit, all that graft sounds exhausting. You have a lot going on right now. Saving money in a current account sounds like a smart and hassle-free move to me.

OPTION TWO: You know you need to grow your money, but you really don't want to spend any more time washing cars. You decide to keep the business running as it is, but it's time to look at other ways to bring some growth. You've heard people talk about investing. An **investment** is when you buy or put your money into something that you believe will increase in value over time, making you more money than you started with. You decide this is the next move for you.

You look at investing in two different types of savings accounts known as **ISA**s and **Premium Bonds**. You might be thinking *Huh?!* at this point, but I'll explain it in detail soon. For the moment, here are the basics. An ISA (*eye-sa*) is an Individual Savings Account, where you earn interest (see page 39) on the money you put into it. You can put in as little as £1 and a maximum of £20,000 a year.

Premium Bonds are similar, but rather than earning interest on the money you put in, each month you have the chance of *winning* money. It works a bit like a **lottery**. The Premium Bonds act as tickets. Loads of tickets are picked each month and if yours is one of them, you win money! And you don't lose any money if you don't win. Your Premium Bonds are still worth the same amount of money and are entered into the next month's prize draw. Each Premium Bond is worth £1, and you can buy anything between £25 and £50,000 worth of them.

You decide Premium Bonds are the right call. You go all in and buy £1,000 worth.

Chen

> I've said it before and I'll say it again – free money, people! Dance with me, Eman. I know it all sounds tiring, Sam, but the way I see it is if you just spend a little bit of time finding the right thing to invest in, you can still chill and make more money. You've worked hard for your money, now your money can work for you. I'd invest the hard-earned cash.

OPTION THREE: You're now making £250 a week and that's mad money. You've worked hard and it's been fun, but it's time to reap the rewards of all your hard work. So you keep the business going and start using my 50-40-10

STUNT OR SAVE

rule (see page 20). From the £1,000 you're now making a month, you save 50 per cent (which is £500), you use 40 per cent (£400) to treat yourself with and you give 10 per cent (£100) to charity each month.

Your first treat is going to the fam. After all, without their bucket and washing-up liquid, you'd never have got your business off the ground! There's an amazing sale on a new smart TV and sound system, reduced from £600 to £400. Time to bring some serious upgrades to your family's home. And in ten months, if you keep up the business and stick to the **50-40-10 RULE**, you'll still hit the £5k target and slowly be on your way to that £1 million goal.

> You know my motto - YOLO! Option three all the way. You've worked looooooong hours to make this money and you deserve to enjoy it. You know, work hard, play hard . . . donate hard! And a brand-new surround sound would be perfect for family movie nights! I'm getting excited just thinking about it! Plus it's not like you're spending all your dough - you'd still make sure you put 50 per cent in your savings account each month.

Ash

A QUICK REALITY CHECK

As you know, we're stretching the rules of the real world in this game so we can educate ourselves and set ourselves up to make the best choices as adults. I like to think that we're playing in **EMAN'S FANTASY FINANCE WORLD** here. What I'm getting at is you can't *actually* put money into most ISAs until you're eighteen or buy Premium Bonds until you're sixteen. But, before you get too upset at missing out on that free money, there are alternatives open to you if you're under sixteen.

If you have some money you would like to invest – maybe you received some birthday money, for example – you can ask your parent or guardian to take out a **JISA** (Junior Individual Savings Account) in your name. With JISAs you can pay in up to £9,000 a year **(IF YOU'RE REALLY LUCKY!)**. Just like with regular ISAs, your money will earn interest. And this money is locked away until you turn eighteen. It's a great way to stop yourself from spending all your cash and waiting for that delayed gratification we talked about.

Or a parent or guardian could buy Premium Bonds for you if you give them your money. If you win one of the monthly payments, the money is transferred to the parent or guardian looking after the bonds for you, and you can decide together what to do with the winnings. You might want to treat yourself to something you've had your eye on, or you could save it, or even buy some more Premium Bonds! Both JISAs and Premium Bonds are great options if you want to start saving now for your future.

EMAN'S ADVICE

OK, OK. That's enough of the real world. Let's step back into my fantasy finance world, and I'll break down the pros and cons of each of our options.

OPTION ONE

I've got a lot of respect for this option. It's important to recognize our limits and when you're feeling tired it's a smart decision not to push yourself any further. If you decide you're already working hard enough and don't want to look into any new options for investing your money, then hats off to you. Only you know which is the best option for you to follow.

Also, there's some smart thinking here.

Do you remember what I was saying about savings way back at the start of the book?

By saving up while you are young, just like I wish I'd done, you're resisting the temptation to spend the cash. If you were to have £120k by the time you're leaving university or just a couple of years after you finish school, you'd be laughing. It's a lot of money.

But here's the weird thing with money – it's worth less over time. So things you can buy with £120,000 today will cost more money in ten years' time. **MAD, RIGHT?** This is called inflation – it's how much the price of an item changes over time.

You might have heard an older relative say something like, 'In my day, you could buy a loaf of bread for 20p, or a house for £20,000.' Well, get this: when I was your age a Freddo chocolate bar was 10p. Can you imagine my surprise when I went into a shop recently and saw it is now 25p? 25p! Shocking! That's a 150 per cent increase in price! At this point, you're probably thinking that I'm ancient, but I'm not – prices are just rising all the time. This happens because the cost of producing things goes up, and therefore the final cost of products goes up too.

Think about all of the things needed to produce the simple (but delicious) Freddo. There are the ingredients – the cacao beans, milk and sugar; the electricity needed to power the factory where they make the chocolate; the plastic for the packaging; and the cost of the wages of the people who make, package and sell it. All of these have increased in price over the years. This also happens because of things like wars and climate change, which make the ingredients and services less easily available. And this then drives the prices up. It's seriously complex stuff, but it's important to know about inflation so you understand why, as you get older, the cost of things you buy daily has risen over time.

You might have heard about something called the **'cost of living crisis'**, which is happening at the time I'm writing this. Currently, people have less money for things they need than they did a couple of years ago. Why? Well, the basic problem is that inflation increased more quickly than it usually does, so the cost of everyday products, such as bread, milk, fish, meat and chocolate, all suddenly increased. So did the price of electricity and fuel.

Added together, this has made everyday life much more expensive. But for lots of people, the money they receive monthly from their jobs – their wages – hasn't increased by the same amount.

This means they can't afford to buy as much as they did a few years ago. It's a very stressful time for a lot of people.

So, while option one is solid, it does mean that the £120k you've saved won't get you the same amount of stuff in ten years' time, and so just saving it up and receiving no interest might not be the best move in the long term.

OPTION TWO

I'm vibing with something Chen said – she's right, you've worked for your money, so now your money can work for you. There really is some truth in this. ISAs and Premium Bonds are a great place to save money that you don't plan to use very often. (Remember, current accounts are for money that you want to access now, whereas savings accounts like these are for the cash you don't use regularly.)

There are different types of ISAs and some of them are riskier than others. With some, such as **cash ISAs**, you will always make more money than you put in. They are a type of savings account where you earn interest without having to pay **tax** on the interest (we'll get on to tax in Chapter Seven).

STUNT OR SAVE

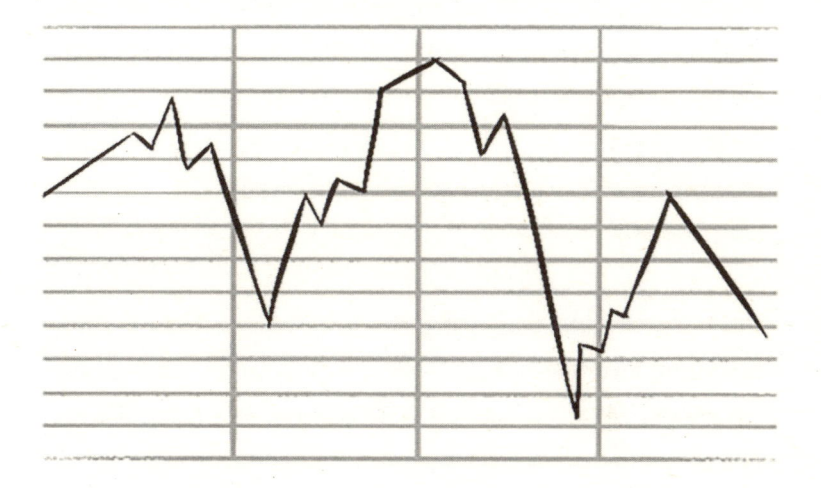

But with others, such as **stocks and shares ISAs**, there's a risk you could lose some of the money you put in because you are investing your money into products and businesses. If they lose money, then you risk losing yours too.

Why take this risk? Because you *can* end up earning a lot more money with a stocks and shares ISA, if what you're investing in is successful.

JUST ONE MORE THING to tell you all about ISAs. The general rule is the longer you keep your money in the ISA, the higher the interest rate and the more money you'll receive.

For example, you *might* receive 2 per cent interest if you put £1,000 into an ISA for one year and make £20 (because £1,000 ÷ 100 (per cent) = £10. £10 x 2 (per cent) = £20). Or you could put £1,000 into an ISA for three years and receive 5 per cent interest. This means you'd make £50 in the first year (£1,000 ÷ 100 (per cent) = £10. £10 x 5 (per cent) = £50).

Premium Bonds work slightly differently. Rather than receiving interest, you're entered into a monthly draw where you might receive money, known as prizes. These prizes are worth between £25 and £1,000,000. If you're lucky enough to receive the £1 million jackpot, then someone called an **'AGENT MILLION'** will visit you to deliver the news in person! Your chances of winning these prizes increase if you own more Premium Bonds. Just like ISAs, you don't pay tax on any rewards you receive. The downside to Premium Bonds is it's not guaranteed that you'll ever win a prize. So you could buy £20,000 worth of Premium Bonds but never win any money.

OK, so now we're all clear about what ISAs and Premium Bonds are, what do I think of option two?

Well, while there's a good chance you'll increase your money with these sorts of investments, there is a possible downside that, by investing in Premium Bonds, you won't ever increase it. But you've been working hard and they are a low-risk option. So at this point on your journey to a million, they're a good shout.

OPTION THREE

I love the thinking here – it's spreading the love and helping those around you, which I'm all about. Plus, if you went with option three, you'd be using my 50-40-10 rule – fist bump! Giving back to your family is a great thing to do too.

But I've got my business hat back on here, so I want to remind you that while I respect your generosity, it's definitely going to slow down your path to the million pound end goal. You'd be going from a sprint to a stroll. Now, I know the 50-40-10 rule is my rule, so you might be thinking,

> Are you telling me I shouldn't be following your rules, Eman?

All I would say is there is a time and place for this rule. And it would be a good idea to have a think about whether this is the right time for such a big gift and whether you really need to be paying yourself and others that much money each month. **CAN YOU REALLY AFFORD IT?** Is it going to be the best way to help you make your million? If the answer is yes, then carry on. If it's no, then maybe cut back on those treats.

THE ULTIMATE GUIDE TO MONEY

MC HAMMER

What would you do if you were rich? And by rich I mean mega rich, superstar-famous rich. The kind of rich where you have millions and millions of pounds in the bank. Maybe you'd get houses, cars, a home cinema and a private jet.

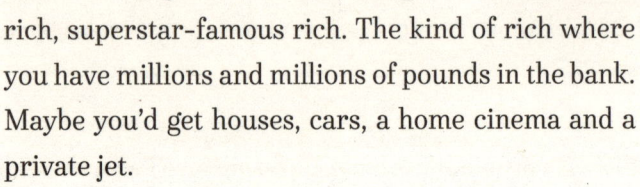

And maybe you would also want your family, friends and people from your community to benefit from your success, so perhaps you'd buy some treats for them too.

You'd live life, enjoy yourself. Who wouldn't?

Well, that's exactly what hip-hop legend MC Hammer did. After making loads of money from his music career, he apparently bought a $30 million house, and spent money on gold-plated gates with 'Hammer Time' written across them (ha!), two swimming pools, a bunch of fancy cars and even a helicopter. He also wanted to bring his community along with him so he hired his friends as staff, but I don't just mean a couple of close mates – at one point he had 200 people working in his mansion, which cost him a million dollars a month (about £1.5 million)!

STUNT OR SAVE

Sadly, this couldn't last forever, and in 1996 he had to file for **bankruptcy**. This is the word for when the amount of money you owe (your debts) is more than the amount of money you have. For example, if you have £1,000 but you owe a bank £10,000, you'd have to declare yourself bankrupt as you don't have enough to pay them back. But your debt doesn't just disappear – the bank will come and repossess (see page 57) your belongings to help pay off the debt. And, after that, borrowing money in the future can be really hard because you're no longer seen by the bank as a reliable person who is able to pay money back. It's a serious business to go bankrupt and can make the rest of your life very difficult.

You might think that MC Hammer regretted his choices and would go back and do things differently, but he doesn't. He told TV host Oprah Winfrey:

> 'I wouldn't change one thing. I really believe in the butterfly effect. Meaning that if I change one thing, everything else changes. I lose the kids I have now. I lose the relationships I have now. I lose the peace I have now. So I'm very happy with my decision.'

And on his journey to peace, MC Hammer went from superstar to super-geek.

He got really interested in technology after making a music video in the 1990s, and as well as continuing to make music, he branched out and started investing his money in technology. In fact, he even put money into X (back when it was still called Twitter) and YouTube when they were still quite new products. He's a great example of not being defeated by things going wrong in life. He's turned things around in an incredible way and he still finds time to tour and perform his music. **WHAT A GUY!**

STUNT OR SAVE

EMAN'S PICK

Have you made your choice?

There's never a quick or easy solution to growing your money, but my choice for this round of the game would be option two – investing in some Premium Bonds. While each option will hit the £5,000 target over time, it's option two that gives you the best chance of increasing your money quickly.

With option one, you aren't making the most of the various opportunities there are out there for **GROWING YOUR MONEY**. And with option three, while it's very generous of you to buy things for your family, it is really going to slow down your journey to a million pounds.

But with option two, you'll definitely reach the target of £5,000 in five months if you carry on your business. And if you're lucky, the Premium Bonds will pay out and help you reach that target even quicker. So either way, you'll hit that goal and maybe even get a little more. Let's see what happens!

Amazing work, you've invested like a pro and made £5,000!

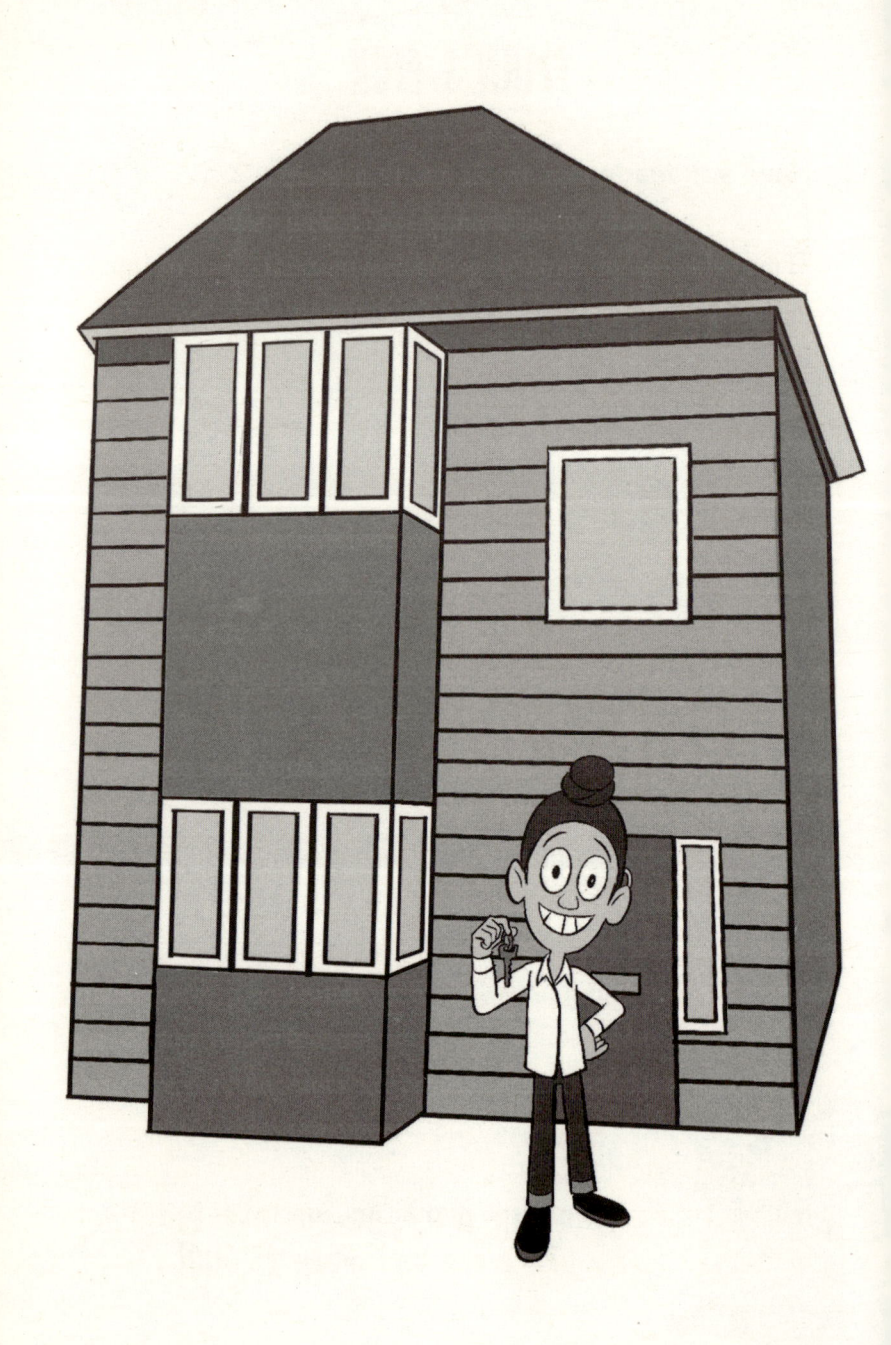

CHAPTER 5
THERE'S NO PLACE LIKE HOME

Let's take a moment to celebrate – you've turned £1 into an impressive £5,000.

It's not always quick to get there – these things take time, patience and work – but you're putting in the effort and it's paying off. I'm proud of you for sticking at it.

KLAXON ALERT

CONGRATULATIONS! YOU'VE WON A PRIZE OF £10,000 FROM PREMIUM BONDS.

Wow, well that investment paid off – and more than we expected! Your cash pot is building up nicely. In fact, it's tripled! Forget £5,000, you're now laughing with £15,000 in the bank.

THE ULTIMATE GUIDE TO MONEY

You have made some impressive choices, even when some of the options have been SUPER tempting, and you've managed to save up some serious cash. I mean I definitely wasn't as smart as you when I was younger. If I'd had £5,000 I wouldn't have been able to find my bed because of all of the new shoeboxes filling up my room. **YOU'RE KILLING IT!**

REALITY CHECK

OK, so I don't want to put a downer on your big win, but I do want to talk about something important. We put £1,000 into Premium Bonds and got lucky: we won £10,000. And sure, this does happen, but I want to get real with you for a moment. The chances that you're going to win that much and that quickly are *quite* low. Premium Bonds are actually a low-risk form of **gambling**.

Gambling is when you spend a certain amount of money on something, whether it's betting on a football game or putting coins into a slot machine, and you hope to get more money in return. But the thing with gambling is that you're not guaranteed to get anything back, including the money you spent in the first place.

THERE'S NO PLACE LIKE HOME

Take slot machines, for example. Slot machines make it seem like you are playing a game. Often the game is that you need to press a button and get three matching symbols on the screen. But you have no control over which symbols come up; it's called a game of chance. It's tempting to play slot machines because if you do match three symbols, you receive a big prize, let's say £100. And it might only cost £1 to have a go. But it's very, very, very unlikely that you'll win. And the problem is, because it doesn't cost very much, people keep playing, and before they know it they've maybe spent £10 or £15 (or a lot more) but received nothing in return. It's not a smart way to spend your money, and it's illegal for under-eighteens in the UK.

Now, with Premium Bonds, you don't lose the money you put in, which is why they're a good thing. But it's still a gamble that you'll win money. So it's great that you lucked out with your Premium Bonds this time but, if you want to get to your goal, you can't just rely on wins like this. You're going to need to put in the work!

RIGHT, BACK TO IT. £15,000 IS A LOT OF MONEY! Think about what you could do with it. Imagine turning up to school kitted out in the coolest designer jacket, fresh shoes and a brand-new bag.

After a week of buying anything you want and treating your friends, you could spend the weekend doing even more shopping, eating at the most luxurious restaurants and visiting amusement parks. You'd feel just like a celebrity! But for how long? This kind of lifestyle could turn your thousands into pennies quickly. Is showing off like this really worth it if it's only temporary?

As we try to grow our money pot to an even bigger amount, I think it's important that we remind ourselves about *why* we make money. The goal for some people is to get as much money as possible, and there's no shame in that. Life without money can be *really* hard. So lots of people feel that the more money they have, the easier, happier and more luxurious their life will be. **I GET THIS.**

But for me, I don't think this should be our main goal. I agree that money can give people a better life in some ways, but I think the motivation should be adding *value* to our lives and the lives of those around us.

What do I mean by value? I mean something good and positive that benefits people. Value is a great thing to focus on rather than the number in a bank account, whether you're making money or spending money.

So, you grow your business in this game, and you go out into the real world, think about ways you can improve your life and the world around you while you do it. Maybe you care about the environment, so you could find a job that helps **PROTECT OUR PLANET**. Or perhaps you're amazing at art, so you could buy some paint and brushes and spend your free time painting murals in hospitals to **BRIGHTEN PEOPLE'S MOODS**. Or maybe you could donate 10 per cent of your money to charity, like I talked about in Chapter One.

Let's keep this in mind as our money grows, and remember to think about how we can add value while we work towards our next goal.

TURN £15,000 INTO £100,000

It's time to turn £15,000 into – wait for it, this one's a big jump – £100,000! It's a huge amount of cash. It could buy you an unforgettable experience with your friends, where you hire out a private yacht and sail around to beautiful islands! But how are we going to make that much dough? Let's remind ourselves of the money we have coming in so far.

We've got our weekend car-washing and phone case business running nicely, bringing in £1,000 a month. And we've invested in (and lucked out with!) Premium Bonds. But we need to do something else to really bump up our pot. We've got a £1 million goal to reach, so we can't be slowing down at this point.

Now it's time to find another **stream of income**. A what? Streams of income are the different ways in which someone can earn money. Have you ever seen a stream flow through a forest? There are parts that break off and flow down different paths, but they are still connected to the main stream. That's what I want you to do. Have income flowing in from different directions, and all coming back to you.

Think about a farm, for example. Often farmers focus on growing crops or raising animals as their main business. But some farmers add other streams of income by renting out fields so people can camp there, or hosting events where visitors can pet and feed their animals. All of these extra things that they do, on top of farming, are different streams of income. Still need convincing? Well, let's take a look at someone who is a boss of multiple income streams.

RIHANNA

Rihanna, the famous singer, songwriter and businesswoman from Barbados, became a global superstar in her teens! As a singer, her job was to record music and perform. She earned a lot of money doing so, but as she got older she wanted to do more than just sing. She noticed that, of all the many make-up products on the shelves, there were tons of different shades for lighter skin tones but there wasn't a range available for darker skin tones. This bothered her, so she decided to create another stream of income by setting up her own make-up brand, Fenty Beauty. Her brand launched with a make-up collection of forty different shades, meaning there is now make-up available for more skin tones than ever before.

INSPIRING, RIGHT? I'm sure people at the time told her to focus on her music. Maybe they wondered why she would even bother to put so much effort into creating a business when she was earning all that money as a musician. However, Fenty Beauty has been incredibly successful and Rihanna has earned much more money from it than her singing. But she hasn't just made loads of money – she's fulfilled a need and added value to the world too, by making darker shades of make-up more easily available. That's my kind of business.

Rihanna's other streams of income are now doing so well that she doesn't have to write songs or perform any more. She's even expanded her business into clothing. Not every part of the business has worked as well, but she's adapted and kept working hard, making her a billionaire in the process! Not sure how much that is? It's a million times a thousand! **IT'S NINE ZEROS – 1,000,000,000!**

YOUR MONEY STREAMS

Has this got you thinking about how you might use Rihanna's story as inspiration to create another stream of income? One thing you could do is invest in a house or flat, which can also be called **property**.

When it comes to having a home, people can do one of two things. They can either buy a property or rent one. Buying a property means it's yours! If you don't have all of the money needed to buy a home, you take out a type of loan from a bank called a mortgage (more on this in a moment). Once you have paid back all of the money borrowed, you own the house (before then, the bank owns part of it and you own part of it). You usually have to keep the mortgage for a minimum amount of time and might get charged quite a lot of money if you pay it off early.

Renting a flat or house means someone else owns the property and you pay them **rent** (or money) each month to live there. If you rent, you don't own any part of the property.

If you're able to buy a property, it's a brilliant way to make money. Firstly, the price of a property usually increases with time. For example, if someone buys a house for £50,000, in ten years' time that house might increase in value and be worth £70,000. This increase in value generally happens because of inflation (see page 74).

THERE'S NO PLACE LIKE HOME

And if someone makes improvements to a property, such as putting in a stylish new kitchen or increasing its size with an extension, it can also make the house worth more money than when it was first bought. This is why buying a property is such a great investment, because often it can be sold for a higher price than it was bought for in the first place.

The second way to make money from property is through rent. If someone owns a house and has a spare bedroom that no one is using, they can rent it out to someone else, known as a **lodger**. Or, they might decide not to live in the property themselves at all, and instead rent out the whole property to people known as **tenants**. Either way, it all creates a source of income for the owner. For example, imagine you own a house that you bought for £100,000 and you rent it out for £1,000 per month.

You would earn £12,000 a year. In ten years' time you would have earned £120,000 (£1,000 x 12 (months) = £12,000. £12,000 x 10 (years) = £120,000). This means you'd have made back the money you paid for the house and gained an extra £20,000 on top of that!

93

Now, you might be wondering how buying a property adds value to your life or the lives of others? Well. If you own a property, you can make it into a happy and safe home for you and your family. And if you own a home but rent out a room or the entire property, you can add value to the lives of others. You see, everyone deserves a home, but not everyone can afford to buy one or to pay rent, because in a lot of places there are real problems with houses being too expensive to buy or the price of rent being too high. So buying a property and creating an affordable space for people to live in can be a great way to add an additional stream of income, while also adding value to others' lives.

How does this relate to us turning £15,000 into £100,000? Well, one of your customers has let you know that there's a three-bedroom house for sale that needs some improvements and repair work, but it's going cheap for £100,000. You decide that it's time to invest in the property market.

When buying a house, you typically pay 10 per cent of the total house price yourself. This is called a **deposit**. So you're going to need to put £10,000 of your money towards this (£100,000 ÷ 100 (per cent) = £1,000. £1,000 x 10 (per cent) = £10,000).

THERE'S NO PLACE LIKE HOME

Then you will need to borrow the rest of the money (£90,000) from the bank. This type of loan is called a mortgage. You'll also need to pay a couple of thousand pounds for a **solicitor**, a person who is trained in dealing with all the legal stuff involved with buying a house. So, from your original £15,000, you'll spend £10,000 on the deposit and £2,000 on legal stuff. This will leave you with £3,000 in the bank to spend as you like.

> **I NEED TO BE STRAIGHT WITH YOU AGAIN.** In the real world, you typically can't get a mortgage until you're eighteen (depending on where in the world you live). But remember, we're stretching reality here, so let's not worry about that!

OK, I know what you're thinking. Borrowing £90,000 from the bank feels like a LOT of money. But don't worry, you don't have to pay it all back in one go. The way mortgages work is you have to pay the bank a certain amount of money each month (over several years) until you've paid it all back. **BUT, THERE IS A CATCH!**

And here it is: you'll have to pay back more money than you borrowed in the first place. That's because a mortgage is a type of loan, and as we know from Chapter Three, you have to pay interest on loans. For your mortgage, the bank sets an interest rate that means you'll pay back £500 a month over twenty-five years.

Now that you've bought your property and you know what it'll cost each month, how are you going to turn your investment into our next goal of £100,000?

YOUR THREE OPTIONS

OPTION ONE: You move into your new pad. (I know, I know, in the real world you're quite a few years off moving out of your family home. But we're living in Eman's fantasy finance world here!) Once you're in, you spend the £3,000 you have in the bank on improving and repairing the property. You add some fresh coats of paint to the walls, lay some new carpets and pay for someone to fix the leaky toilet. It's looking great already! These improvements and repairs mean people will be more likely to want to live there.

You decide to rent out your two spare bedrooms to your older sibling and a cousin, for £500 a month each – they'll become your lodgers. (Most rooms cost a little bit more, but you think it's important people can afford to pay their rent so you keep the cost of yours a bit lower – plus they're family!) Between your car washing (£1,000 a month) and the rent (£500 x 2 = £1,000 a month), you earn £2,000 a month in total. After paying the mortgage (£500) and your share of the bills (£100), you put the remaining £1,400 in the bank. (£2,000 (income) - £600 (mortgage + bills) = £1,400). After two years you plan on selling your much-improved property and hopefully making a big profit.

Chen

> You know what, I quite like the idea of living with some new people, even if they are family. I'd totally go for this option. Plus, my cousin is amazing at cooking so I won't have to eat cheese on toast every night for dinner. Hopefully your cousin has some secret chef skills too!

OPTION TWO: You're making good money with the car washing, so you decide to move out of your parents' house and start living by yourself. With the £1,000 you earn each month, you pay for the mortgage (£500 a month) and bills (£300 a month – because you live alone, you have to pay all the bills yourself, unlike in option one) and this leaves you with £200 a month to save (£1,000 (car-washing earnings) - £800 (mortgage + bills) = £200). You even manage to fill your home with free bits of furniture people were just going to throw away. After two years you hope inflation will mean that you'll be able to sell the house for a profit.

THE ULTIMATE GUIDE TO MONEY

Ash

> Nah, forget lodgers, even if they are family. I'd pick living solo. Your mates could crash in the spare room when you have mega games nights.

OPTION THREE: You've seen enough home-improvement programmes to know all about this thing called 'flipping' houses – that's buying them, doing improvements and repairs, and selling them again quickly. You decide to use your £1,000 a month from the car washing to cover the mortgage and bills (£500 + £300 = £800) and fix up as much of the house as you can. You watch a lot of YouTube how-to videos and spend each Sunday at the house learning how to paint rooms, hang wallpaper, put new tiles in the bathroom and fix dripping taps. After just three months you're ready to flip this thing.

Sam

> I would SO go for the flipping option. It's the fastest way to make the cash! It'd be hard work, but that wouldn't scare me off – think of the new skills you'd learn. Plus my grandma and I love watching these renovation programmes on TV. She gets so much joy from seeing people turn sad white rooms into colourful spaces.

THERE'S NO PLACE LIKE HOME

EMAN'S ADVICE

OPTION ONE

OK, I see what's happening. You're already putting my lessons into practice – EXCELLENT WORK, MY FRIEND. It's great to see you thinking about how to add value to both your life and other people's. Looking after the lodgers, even if they are family, and the property's finances is going to take time though, and it's a lot of responsibility. If something goes wrong, you'll need to fix it. If someone moves out, you'll need to find a new lodger quickly. Otherwise, you'll need to pay out more of your own money on the mortgage. There are risks, but I like your approach.

OPTION TWO

Good idea to look at what furniture you can get for free! I like where your head's at here. But it's your monthly numbers that worry me. You make £1,000 a month with your car-washing business, and your mortgage and bills come to £800. What if you have a quiet two weeks and don't wash any cars for a couple of weekends in a row and only earn £700 that month? Then you won't be able to afford your mortgage and bills! We've seen the risks of not being able to pay back loans, and the same goes for mortgages. And because you're only saving £200 a month (£1,000 (car-washing earnings) - £800 (mortgage + bills) = £200 (savings)), you'll need to sell your property for a big profit to hit that £100k target.

OPTION THREE

My young entrepreneur – your enthusiasm is exactly what I like to see. Your plan is great, but you didn't pay close attention to the small print when you signed up for the mortgage. Part of your mortgage agreement says that you've agreed to pay it back for a minimum of two years. This means that if you want to sell your property early, say after one year, you'll have to pay an **early exit fee** of £2,500, which would affect your profits.

KLAXON ALERT

> AFTER THREE MONTHS YOUR BOILER BREAKS... AND IT'S WINTER! THERE'S NO HOT WATER OR HEATING IN YOUR HOUSE AND IT'S FREEZING! YOU NEED TO REPAIR IT PRONTO! THAT'LL SET YOU BACK £3,000. TIME TO PAY UP.

Ugh, so this is what it's really like to own a home. It's not always as simple as a stack of cash coming your way; sometimes it means paying for unexpected things. Whether it's a broken boiler, electricity bills increasing or food prices going up because of inflation, life can throw you financial curveballs at times. This is why having savings is important. When unexpected things happen, people can end up having to take out expensive loans to help pay to fix the problem. The best thing to do is keep ahead of the game and put some money to one side for curveballs like this. Some of these options left you with money to save, but some of them didn't.

Now you've read my advice and had a glimpse into the future with that dodgy boiler, it's your last chance to make your decision. **WHAT OPTION WOULD YOU CHOOSE TO MAKE THE £100,000?**

EMAN'S PICK

I think investing in a property that isn't in the best state is a great investment. Why? Because you can improve it, then sell it for more than you bought it for after you've had it long enough to avoid being hit with an early exit fee. But of all the options here, I think your best bet is option one. There are definitely some risks with this plan, but you've made some smart choices by not pricing the rent too high and by hanging on to some spare cash to cover any unexpected problems, such as that broken boiler. The risks with options two and three are much higher because you might either not make enough money each month to pay your mortgage and bills, or you might not be able sell the property for enough money to reach your target.

Option one is what I'd do. But let's look into my crystal ball and see how options two and three might have stacked up in the end once the property hit the market.

Let's start with the runner-up – Sam's pick of option three, to flip the property. After three months and your best repair efforts, your house sold for £20,000 profit. You managed to keep your savings at £3,000 by putting the leftover car-wash money back into your savings, but you then had to spend it all on the new boiler. So there's currently £20,000 in your account (£20,000 (profit) + £3,000 (savings) - £3,000 (new boiler) = £20,000). And you still need to pay that exit fee of £2,500 for ending your mortgage early, so that quickly drops to £17,500 (20,000 (total profit) - £2,500 (early exit fee) = £17,500). It's not a bad effort, especially in just three months, and it would have been more if not for the broken boiler that required skill way beyond a YouTube tutorial. It's good going, but it's a long way shy of the £100,000 goal.

In third place, we have Ash's favourite, option two. After two years, you move back in with your parents and put the house on the market. The cost of the boiler used all of your savings, and the little bit of money you had left over each month after paying your bills has meant you weren't able to do any renovations on the place. It's looking pretty shabby from two years of use and all those gaming nights you and your mates had. Still, it has increased in value because of inflation and you sell it for £40,000 profit. **NICE GOING**, but you'd still be pretty far from the £100,000 target.

AND SO THE WINNER IS OPTION ONE! Are you celebrating with Chen? Don't worry if you're not –

investing in property can be a tricky business. This was a smart option because saving that extra cash from your lodgers each month meant you were able to buy a new boiler and fast, so your lodgers were happy and warm. When you take into account the £3,000 you spent on home improvements when you bought the house, after two years (and that new boiler) you saved up a whopping £27,600 (£1,400 (monthly savings) x 24 months = £33,600 (total savings). £33,600 (total savings) - £3,000 (new boiler) - £3,000 (repairs and decorating) = £27,600 profit).

You decide to hang on to £20,000 of those savings, move back home with your parents and spend £7,000 putting in a new kitchen, a new bathroom and even more new carpets before you sell the house. All that investment into the property pays off and you sell it for £80,000 profit. Add that to the savings you've got in the bank (£20,000) and you've got yourself £100,000 (£80,000 (house sale profit) + £20,000 (savings) = £100,000). And there we have a clear winner.

High five, you've climbed the property ladder and reached £100,000!

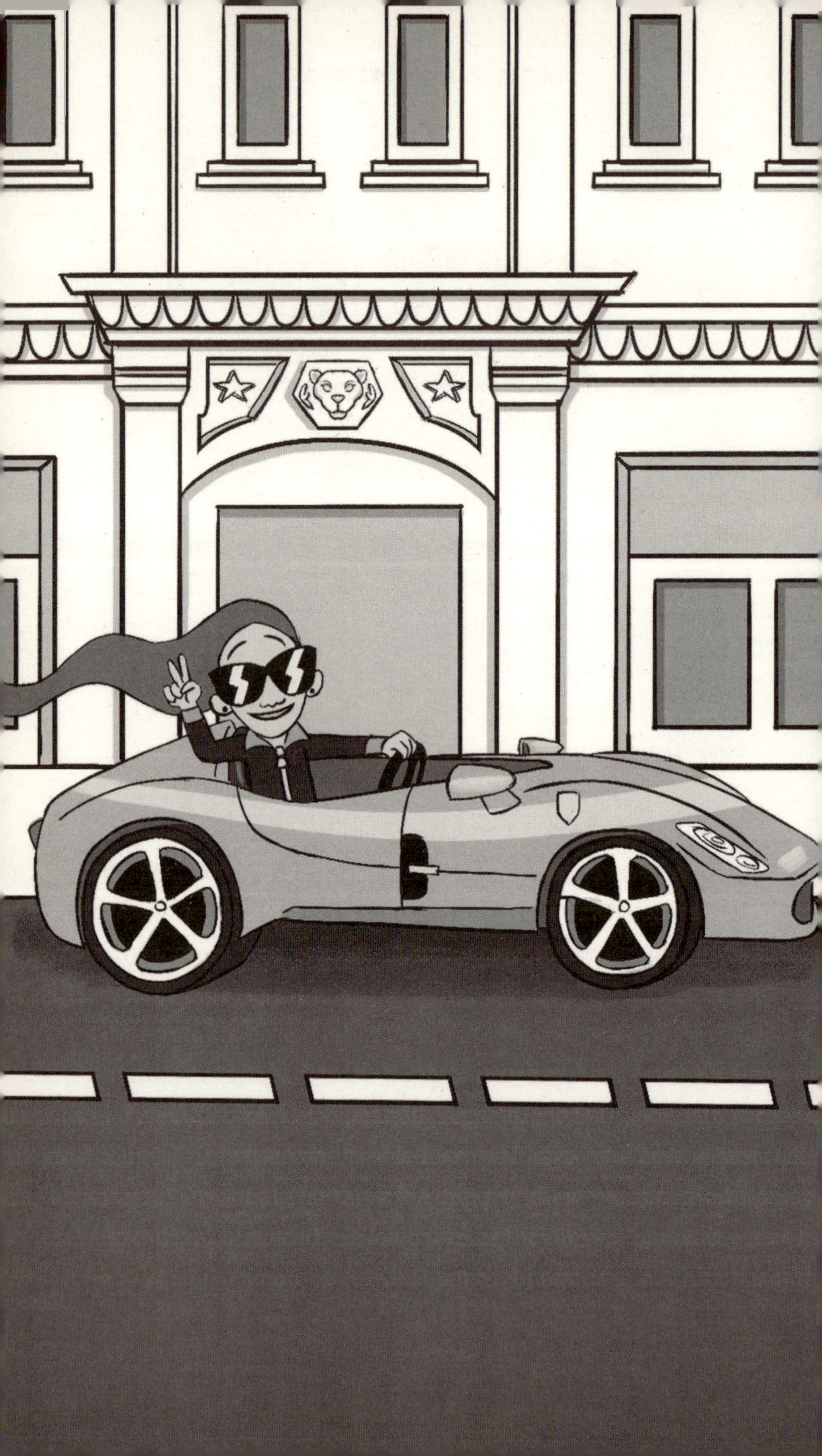

CHAPTER 6
SHOW ME THE MONEY!

Oh my days – £100k! That's some serious money . . . we've left the world of sweets and Freddos far behind us.

We're on to bigger things now! Think luxury trips around the world, all the clothes you've ever wanted and VIP experiences everywhere you go! But can you make even more and grow it to £500k? **THAT'S HALF A MILLION POUNDS!** And yep, that means that if you hit this, you'll be halfway to your goal! It's SO much money. Forget taking out a mortgage from a bank; you could buy a whole house with that much money, and you'd even have enough spare change to buy a super-impressive sports car!

Half a million is a big ask. You've made a tidy profit from branching out into property, and your car-washing and phone case businesses are continuing to bring in some good money. But those are baby steps compared to what's to come.

It's time to play with the big bucks.

BUYING AND SELLING SHARES

We're going to look at buying and selling shares. I know, I know. It all sounds a bit serious and grown up but let me break it down for you. Some companies are owned by lots of different people, rather than being owned by one person. If you want to own a part of a company then you need to pay some money to buy part of it. The parts of the company you buy are called shares.

Think of a company like a cake. Someone might own all of the cake. Or they might decide the cake is too big to keep all to themselves, so they cut the cake up into slices and sell each slice. Anyone who wants some of this cake can buy a slice, or a share, of the cake. Now everyone who has a piece is known as a **shareholder** of that cake.

The main reason people buy shares is to make money. But you can't just pop down to your local supermarket and buy some shares in a company along with a bar of chocolate and a magazine. You have to buy them from a different type of market – the stock market (or a stock exchange).

Just like there are lots of supermarkets, there are lots of stock markets too. There's the London Stock Exchange (LSE), the New York Stock Exchange (NYSE) and the Shanghai Stock Exchange (SSE), to name just a few. Companies usually sell their shares on the stock market that is based in the same country as they are. For example, a company based in Glasgow would sell their shares on the London Stock Exchange since they're both in the UK. But a company based in Cape Town in South Africa would sell their stocks on the Johannesburg Stock Exchange (JSE) since it's also in South Africa.

OK, so now we know what shares are and where to buy them, the next thing we need to know is *how* to buy them. The thing is, you can't just stroll into the London Stock Exchange and pick up a couple of shares. You have to buy shares from a **stockbroker** or a **platform** instead. A stockbroker is a person who buys and sells shares on the stock market for other people. A platform is an app or a website that you can use to buy shares. You can buy shares through either. Both will likely charge you a fee for their service.

SO HOW MUCH DOES A SHARE COST? Well this *really* varies.
Buying a share in one company might be like buying part of a Freddo, so these shares cost just pennies because a Freddo isn't worth very much. But buying shares in a different company might be like buying a part of a house, which is worth a lot. So these shares could cost hundreds or even thousands of pounds each!

You don't just have to buy shares from one company though; you can own shares in lots of different companies. And how many shares you buy all depends on how much money you want to spend. For example, you could buy 100 shares in one company or 20 shares in five different companies. It's completely up to you.

The next question is how do you actually make money from shares? Well, there are two main ways. If the company you own a part of is doing well, and lots of people are buying their products or using their services, they will make a profit. And as a shareholder of a company, you will get a portion of the company's profits. This is called a **dividend**.

The other way to make money from shares is by selling them, which you can also do via a stockbroker or on a platform. The aim when selling shares is usually to sell them for a higher price than you bought them for. So say I buy 100 shares in a company for £1 each, it means I have invested £100 in that company. If I then sold them a year later for, for example, £3 each, I would have sold my shares for £300 (£3 (share price) x 100 (number of shares) = £300). But remember, I haven't made £300 – I have to take away the original money I invested, which was £100. So I've made £200 profit (because £300 - £100 = £200).

This might have you asking, 'Why does the price of the shares go up?'. The price of shares goes up and down because of things known as **supply** and **demand**. Think about ice lollies.

SHOW ME THE MONEY!

On a really hot summer's day, there's nothing better than enjoying an ice-cold lolly. **(WHAT'S YOUR FAVOURITE? ME, I LOVE A FRUIT PASTILLE ICE LOLLY.)** But have you ever gone into a shop on a scorching-hot day and found the freezer section empty because they've sold out of ice lollies? That's because everyone else wanted an ice lolly too. The lollies were in high demand, but the supply was low, because everyone else had already bought them. In fact, I bet you were so desperate for an ice lolly that you would have paid more money than you normally would to get your hands on one.

But there are also times when ice lollies are in low demand. Like when it's cold in the winter. Most people don't want frozen liquid on a stick when it's snowing outside – they want a hot drink. And during the colder months there are normally loads of ice lollies in the freezer section – so there's a high supply but a low demand. And because there's a low demand, no one is going to pay more than normal for an ice lolly. **MAKE SENSE?**

This is how shares work. When there's a high demand for them, but a low supply, people will pay more. This is when the price of a share goes up – because lots more people want to get their hands on it. But when there's a low demand, like the ice lollies in winter, and the supply is high, the price goes down because no one is that bothered about having any.

So what makes the demand go up? Unfortunately, it's not quite as simple as a hot or cold day. All sorts of things can change how much people are willing to pay for shares, such as when a company launches a new product or service, or how easily available the products are.

OK, so there's one last important thing I need to tell you about. When you buy shares in a company you can either make a **high-risk investment** or a **low-risk investment**. A high-risk investment is when there's a greater chance of losing the money you invest. But the reason people do it is because if the investment goes well, you could make a boatload of money.

A low-risk investment is one that means you're less likely to lose your money, but you probably won't increase your money by a huge amount. We've actually already come across a low-risk investment – Premium Bonds. They are low-risk because you don't lose any of the money you put into them. But as we discussed, the chances of making lots of money from them is limited.

SHOW ME THE MONEY!

So why are some investments high-risk and others low-risk? Well, when it comes to buying shares, a lot of it comes down to how confident people are that a company is going to do well or not.

Let's think about this with chocolate. **WHAT'S YOUR FAVOURITE CHOCOLATE BAR?** Mine's a Cadbury Dairy Milk bar. In fact, lots of people like Cadbury chocolate, and Cadbury have been selling chocolate bars for years and years. Because so many people like and eat their chocolate, the company who produce Cadbury make a profit each year. For this reason, buying shares in Cadbury would be a low-risk investment because it's already such a successful company.

But let's say I start a new company (often called a **start-up**) that sells chocolate. I might call it Eman's Chocolate Drops and sell chocolate in the shape of raindrops filled with caramel - yum! I start telling people how amazing my chocolate is and they get excited and want to buy shares in my company. **GREAT NEWS!** The shares would be cheap, as I'm a new company. But this would be a high-risk investment because I'm a new business, and we don't know how much chocolate I'm going to sell. People might not like my chocolate or might prefer to buy chocolate they already know. If my sales were low, my company wouldn't make a profit, and the people who bought shares wouldn't receive a dividend. It also means that if they wanted to sell their shares in my chocolate company, no one would be interested in buying them, because there wouldn't be a demand for my chocolate. (Sad times. But more chocolate for me!) If this happened, the people who bought the shares would end up losing money.

But what if everyone loved my chocolate? Well, then I might start selling it in all the big supermarkets, and my company would start making a profit.

Suddenly, lots more people would want to buy shares in it, and there would now be a high demand for those shares. And if there was a high demand, the price of the shares would go up. So the people who bought shares in the early days, when they were cheap, would now be able to sell them for loads more money because the demand would have increased. If this happened, their high-risk investment would have paid off because they would have made more money than they first spent!

SHOW ME THE MONEY!

It doesn't stop there though. What if Cadbury came along and decided to buy *my* chocolate company for LOADS of money because they wanted Eman's Chocolate Drops to be part of their business? This would be amazing news for my shareholders for two reasons. Firstly, they would receive some of this money from Cadbury via a dividend. And secondly, because Eman's Chocolate Drops would now be owned by Cadbury, who everyone agrees is a low-risk investment, the share price would go up even more. So shareholders would be able to sell their shares for a **BUCKETLOAD OF CASH**!

Some people spend a lot of time researching small companies and trying to work out which ones have the potential to become really successful. If you can predict which companies have the potential to grow and become profitable, you can buy shares, and see that investment turn to profit! Big brands like Microsoft, Amazon and Sony all started out as small businesses (in the early days, Microsoft was run from a garage!) and eventually grew into huge companies. And anyone who bought cheap shares in these companies when they were small will have been able to sell the shares for a lot more than they bought them for once the companies became successful.

There are always new things coming out and people hoping to create the next big thing. Maybe one day you'll spot a business that you believe is worth your investment. Remember, you have to be over eighteen to invest in stock, but in the meantime you can invest via a Junior ISA.

CRYPTOCURRENCIES

One of the most popular investments in recent years has been **cryptocurrencies**, which definitely sounds like something from the future. Now I know a lot of people struggle to get their head around these, but if you stick with me, I'll explain it for you! Cryptocurrencies are digital forms of money. Unlike the money we are used to, there are no coins or notes for cryptocurrencies, and people can make payments without even having to use a bank. **CLEVER, RIGHT?** In 2009, Bitcoin, a type of cryptocurrency, was launched. Since then thousands of different types of cryptocurrencies have been created.

You can't hold cryptocurrencies in your hand. You can only see them in a digital wallet, or on a **blockchain**, which is a type of digital graph that lists all the things you've paid for with a cryptocurrency. Think of a blockchain like a piece of LEGO. Every purchase is an individual block of LEGO that stacks up to create a final shape, like a car or a house. But instead of a car or a house, a blockchain creates a picture showing a list of everything you've bought.

Cryptocurrencies can only be spent in the digital world. You know how in some online games or apps you can win tokens or 'coins' when you win each round? This is not real money – they're just tokens within the game. Even if you

SHOW ME THE MONEY!

buy extra tokens with real-life money, you still wouldn't be able to go and use the tokens from the game to buy snacks from your local shop. **TRY BUYING SWEETS IN REAL LIFE WITH YOUR CANDY CRUSH WINNINGS OR ROBUX AND SEE WHAT HAPPENS!** And it's the same for cryptocurrencies.

Investing in shares or cryptocurrencies can be a great way to make money. But they can be risky investments, so it's important to do lots of research and understand exactly how big the risk is before you make any decisions.

SO WHERE SHOULD I INVEST MY MONEY?

Before you start investing, you need to decide how much money you want to invest. Now that you've stacked up £100k, you need to think very carefully about the risks you take from now on because you don't want to lose all of that money. Think back to when we had £100. I know, it feels like years ago! Our aim was to turn that £100 into £1,000. We spent almost all of the money we had on supplies to grow the car-washing business. We did the same when we put £1,000 into Premium Bonds and £12,000 of our £15,000 into buying a house. Each time, we chose to spend almost all of our money. It was a risk, but it paid off. But it took so much time and hard work to make the £100,000 we have now. Think about it – if we had lost the £100 because our investment hadn't paid off, it would have been a lot easier to make back £100 than £100,000!

So now that you have a much larger sum, I'm not going to suggest you invest all of it. Instead, you can invest a smaller amount and still increase your overall money pot. You currently have £100,000 from selling the house, and so I think that investing around 30 per cent of your money would be a good idea. That would mean investing £30,000 (because £100,000 ÷ 100 (per cent) = £1,000. £1,000 x 30 (per cent) = £30,000). The problem with investing a lower number,

SHOW ME THE MONEY!

say £10,000, is that it will be harder to reach the target of £500,000. And if you invest a much higher amount, say £70,000, the risk of losing almost all of your hard-earned money is higher.

This way, even if the investment doesn't work out and you lose the £30,000, you'd still have £70,000 in the bank (because £100,000 - £30,000 = £70,000). Keep this in mind as you look over the options below. **WHICH DO YOU THINK IS THE BEST ONE TO GET YOU TO YOUR GOAL?**

YOUR THREE OPTIONS

OPTION ONE: Seeing as it's your first time investing in the stock market, you decide to play it as safe as you can, and choose to invest in some low-risk stocks. You buy shares in six companies that have been around for a while and have a good track record. You invest £30,000 by buying 5,000 shares in each company for £1 each (5,000 (shares) x £1 = £5,000. £5,000 x 6 (companies) = £30,000).

Chen

I like the sound of investing in big, old companies. Surely that's the safer option, right? You've worked too long and too hard to get this far, so no way do I think you should jeopardize it all on something risky. Keep building towards your goal, but slow and steady, pound by pound.

You feel you've invested wisely, without risking it all, and you'll still be making £12,000 a year from the car-washing business. As it's a low-risk opportunity, the money will eventually come in, but it will take a while to reach the goal – probably at least three years.

OPTION TWO: You decide to take a riskier option and hope for a bigger payout. After keeping an eye on several different companies, you buy £30,000 worth of shares in a new tech **start-up** business that you've researched. This leaves you with £70,000 in savings in the bank. The business is doing something that no other tech company is doing, and lots of people seem to be very excited about it! You buy 120,000 shares at 25p each – because it's new, the shares aren't too expensive (120,000 (shares) x 25p = £30,000). You're hoping the company will be bought quite quickly by a bigger tech company, such as Microsoft, so you can sell your shares for a lot more money in a year's time. They will need to go up a lot in value before you can sell them to reach your goal – it's a risk, but you're hoping it will pay off.

SHOW ME THE MONEY!

Sam

I think you're being a little too cautious, Chen. Be bold! I'd do the work and research and invest in a new company. Plus it's exciting, being involved in a new start-up business. Even though I'm new to all of this shares stuff, I think investing in a new company seems fun – it would make me sound like I know what I'm talking about.

OPTION THREE: You're not here to play. You want to be part of the future and this cryptocurrency thing sounds like the money of the future to you. You go big and from the £100,000, you invest £60,000 in Bitcoin (leaving you with £40,000 in the bank). Yep, that's right, you're investing 60 per cent of your money (£100,000 ÷ 100 (per cent) = £1,000. £1,000 x 60 (per cent) = £60,000). Bitcoins are expensive at £15,000 each, so you can only afford four of them (£15,000 x 4 = £60,000). Even with all the other money you have coming in and the savings in your bank, you'll need to sell them for a whopping £115,000 each to reach your goal. You *really* need their value to increase.

Ash

I'm loving the sound of this futuristic LEGO brick money business. My vote is crypto, my friend. Go big or go home, I say.

EMAN'S ADVICE

There's a lot to think about here and the thing with these types of investments is that nothing is ever guaranteed. If it was, then we'd all be gazillionaires! But sadly, it doesn't work like that. Very clever people and huge companies spend A LOT of time and money trying to figure out when the price of shares will go up and when they'll go down, or which companies are going to increase in value and which are going to decrease. So we can't say for certain which is the best option to make you money here. What we can do is look at the pros and cons and weigh up the risks of each.

OPTION ONE

This option is definitely the more cautious of the three, because you're investing across six different companies. The pro is that if one company happens to make lower profits and you get lower dividends from it, then you still have five other companies that you've bought shares in that could help make up the difference. This means you could still earn a nice sum from the dividends even if all of the companies don't do amazingly well. The con is that these are all well-established companies who typically have lots and lots of shareholders, so it's unlikely that you'll get lots and lots of money each time the dividends pay out (compared to a smaller, newer company with fewer shareholders). Basically, it'll probably take a little longer to hit the target, but you should get there eventually.

OPTION TWO

OK, I like the work, time and research that has gone into this idea. And one of the real positives of investing in an up-and-coming company is that there's the potential of making some serious money. The risk with this option is that you've put all of your eggs in one basket. In other words, you've put all of your hope into just one company. If this company doesn't do as well as you expect, you've got no backup option. It might not be bought by a bigger company and the shares might never increase in value. Worse still, they could even go down in price, meaning you'd *lose* money. While there's an opportunity to win big, there's also a possibility you'll lose big with this high-risk investment.

OPTION THREE

You might have noticed that buying cryptocurrency is A LOT more expensive than buying shares. This is because there's often a limited amount (or supply) of certain cryptocurrencies, such as Bitcoin, available. This is also why the price can increase so much – there's a limited supply, but demand can be high.

The biggest pro of buying cryptocurrencies is there's the potential for seriously high rewards. But they're a much newer type of investment, and much riskier. You see, a company usually provides products or services that people will pay for. For example, Coca-Cola makes a drink that people buy and Amazon has its shopping and streaming service that people can sign up for. As long as people still want these products or services, the company should make a profit and its shareholders will earn money.

Also, these companies have to send out reports to prove how much money they're making and spending. This information is all checked to make sure it's correct and no one is lying. It's known as being **regulated**. What this means is that these companies can't pretend they're making more profit than they really are. It also means you can check these reports to help you decide whether it's a good company to invest in or not.

SHOW ME THE MONEY!

CRYPTOCURRENCIES DON'T WORK LIKE THAT. They're not selling a product or service that you can use in the real world. This means that if everyone suddenly decides they're not worth anything, the demand goes away and they are worthless, meaning you lose your money.

Think of it like this. Imagine I am selling a loaf of bread, and I believe it is worth £1,000 so I charge customers that much for it. Customers buy it, and soon other people agree that this is its value, and so they also go out and buy loaves of bread for £1,000. But a bit later someone else comes along and says we're all being silly; a loaf of bread is clearly only worth 45p. And then everyone agrees with them and decides bread is only worth 45p. This means the price suddenly drops by looooads! I mean, who's going to buy a loaf of bread for £1,000 when it's widely believed it's worth 45p?

> Well, cryptocurrencies are a bit like bread – it's all based on what people think they're worth.

They are also **unregulated**, which means there is no one checking to see if what they are saying the cryptocurrencies are worth is true! People have to buy them based on trust. But if people suddenly lose this trust, this is another moment when the value of a cryptocurrency can really drop.

For me, I also think 60 per cent is a bit too much to be investing because the risk is too high. It'd be a lot of money to lose that you've worked very hard to make. I think for this part of the game, the sweet spot is to invest more like 30 per cent of your income. Option three would be a *very* risky move . . .

NFTs

Cryptocurrencies can be hard to get your head around. Everyone knows they can't be used in the physical world, but still, lots of people have 'agreed' that they are valuable for some reason. All of this agreeing has created a demand for something that you can't really use. And as I've said, the problems really start when everyone changes their mind and decides, actually, they're not that interested in them after all.

This is exactly what happened with **NFTs** (or 'non-fungible tokens'). NFTs are a type of cryptocurrency. Each NFT is represented by a digital image – a picture, basically – which is one-of-a-kind and can't be copied or stolen.

Think of them like a digital passport – each one is different and unique to their owner. But rather than keeping them in a bank or in your house, NFTs are stored on a blockchain – remember those LEGO bricks we spoke about on page 114?

SHOW ME THE MONEY!

It's thought that the first NFT was created in 2014. By 2021 people were very excited by them and they were worth A LOT of money, so people quickly started investing in them, and more and more were created. Canadian pop star Justin Bieber apparently paid almost £1 million for Bored Ape #3001 in 2022 (no prizes for guessing what the picture representing this NFT looked like!). But as more NFTs were created, the demand began to go down – they became too easily available! And so their value dropped too. So what happened to Justin's investment? **HE LOST A LOT OF MONEY.** By July 2023, Bored Ape #3001 was worth just £45,000! That's a loss of £955,000!

While this wasn't ideal, Justin didn't have to worry too much because he was still making money from his music and his clothing company, Drew House. But it's a perfect example of why investing in something new, such as cryptocurrencies, can be so risky.

EMAN'S PICK

So, I think I've made it pretty clear by this point that option three is not for me. It's a BIG investment using 60 per cent of your money and a pretty risky one at that. But I can see the value in options one and two, and I think both are good choices. So if you picked one of those, we're starting to think the same!

If I *had* to pick, I'd go for option two. Why? Because it involves investing a sensible amount of your money – 30 per cent – and it has the potential to grow and make you a profit much faster. Option one will mean it takes you a while to get to the goal of £500,000, and we've still got to double our money after that to reach a million. So while option one isn't a bad decision, I'm choosing to focus on speed here.

So, let's take another look in my crystal ball and see if my pick gets us to our goal . . .

The investment was risky, but it paid off! Your research was on the money! The tech company was bought by a much larger company, pushing the price of the shares up. You sold your shares and after paying a fee to the stockbroker, you earned £3.50 for each share you bought. This means you earned £420,000 after just twelve months (£3.50 (share price) x 120,000 (number of shares) = £420,000). If you add

SHOW ME THE MONEY!

that to the £70,000 you had in the bank and the £12,000 you made from washing cars and selling phone cases over the past year, you're sitting on £502,000 (£420,000 + £70,000 + £12,000 = £502,000)!! **EXCELLENT WORK.**

Smart investments, my friend. You've made £500,000! You're halfway there!

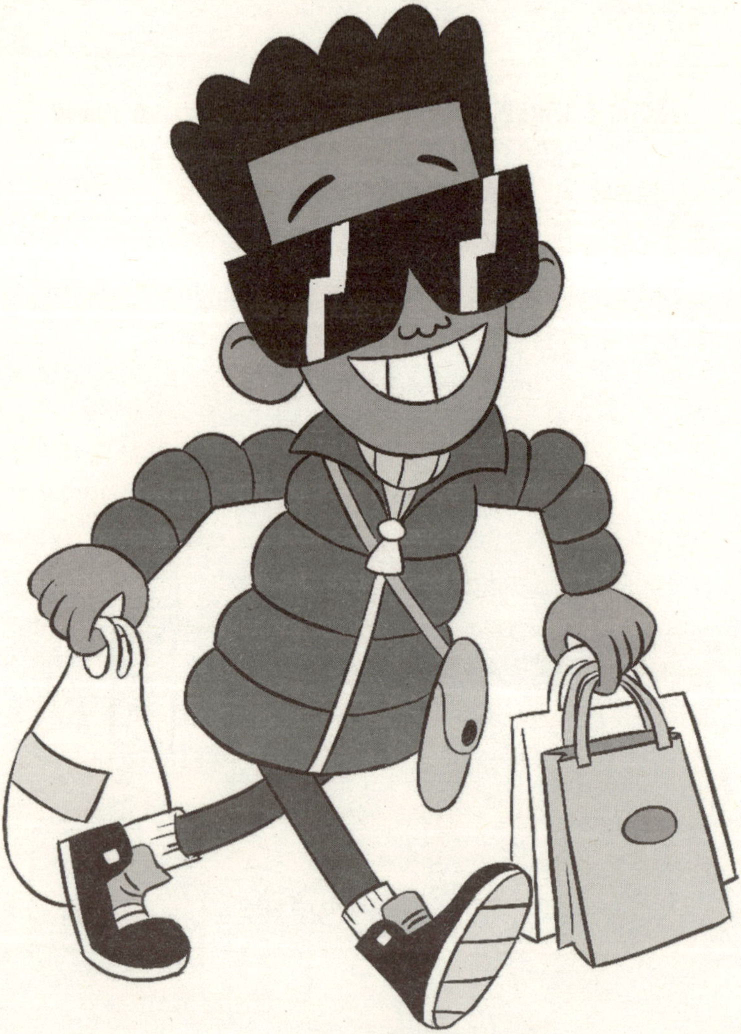

CHAPTER 7
SO, YOU WANT TO BE A MILLIONAIRE?

We've made it – there's only one more decision between you and a million pounds! Did you think you would make it this far when you started with just a single pound coin? I didn't doubt you for a second. You've worked so hard, learned so much, taken some big risks but also been smart with your money. And wow, has it paid off. Five hundred thousand pounds is sitting in the bank. Are you tempted to spend some of it, or are you going to tap into that delayed gratification one more time and take the final leap to a million? Let's find out . . .

KLAXON ALERT

YOU OWE THE GOVERNMENT £73,000 IN TAX ON YOUR EARNINGS.

You've made a lot of money in the last year, but this means you need to pay tax. Tax is the word for money that workers and businesses have to pay to the government. It is illegal not to pay taxes. The money is used to fund public services. These change depending on which country you live in, but taxes can pay for things like hospitals, schools and rubbish collection.

In the UK, tax is paid by people and businesses who earn more than £1,000 a month. The more a worker earns, the more tax they have to pay.

There are two types of tax: **direct tax** and **indirect tax**. **Income tax** is a direct tax, which means it is taken directly from a person or business's earnings and goes straight to the government. Some countries, such as Bahrain and Kuwait, don't have income tax, but most countries in the world do.

Indirect tax is the money that is added to products we buy. For example, if I went into a bakery in the UK and bought a gingerbread man, the price I'd pay for it would include something called **Value Added Tax** (VAT) – a type of indirect tax. In some countries, such as India and Australia, this indirect tax is known as the Goods and Services Tax (GST). The bakery will receive the VAT from the customer, then pay this on to the government. And this is why it is called an indirect tax – it

SO, YOU WANT TO BE A MILLIONAIRE?

is not paid by you to the government directly; instead, it goes from the customer to the supplier to the government. The next time you buy something, have a look at the receipt and you'll see how much VAT you have paid.

So since you've earned £420,000 this year from your investments, you need to pay something called **capital gains tax** on that money. Capital gains tax is another type of direct tax. In the UK, when you make money from selling something that has increased in value, such as a second home or shares, you owe the government money in the form of capital gains tax. I'll save you all the maths – the short answer is, you owe the government £73,000!

UGH, THAT WAS A BIT UNEXPECTED, RIGHT? And it's dropped

our bank balance down to £429,000 (£502,000 - £73,000 = £429,000). But tax is a part of life and, depending on where you are in the world, paying taxes towards public services means everyone, no matter how rich or poor they are, has the same access to important services, from healthcare to clean streets. In the UK, it means you can see a doctor, get an operation, have your recycling collected and receive an education without paying anything (unless you choose to go private), because it's all paid for by money from taxes.

Now, although we need to get that number back up to £500k before doubling our money to hit the big million, I think it's time to have a little bit of fun first. You've been working hard, saving, investing, researching, putting in a lot of shifts car washing and decorating I don't know how many phone cases. So, it's time to have a break. It's very important to remember one of the big reasons why we earn money – it's to bring extra value to our lives. **TO ENJOY OURSELVES!**

> You've got £9,000 to spend. What do you want to do?

YOUR THREE OPTIONS

OPTION ONE: You go on an amazing holiday with your family and bring along a couple of friends too. You'll stay on a private island in incredible wood huts where you can step right out on to a white sandy beach. You'll be able to snorkel in crystal-clear waters with fish so colourful you won't believe your eyes, build sandcastles the size of your bed and do loads of fun action-packed activities in the rainforest. Oh, and the ice-cream is **UNLIMITED**. It's heaven and worth every penny.

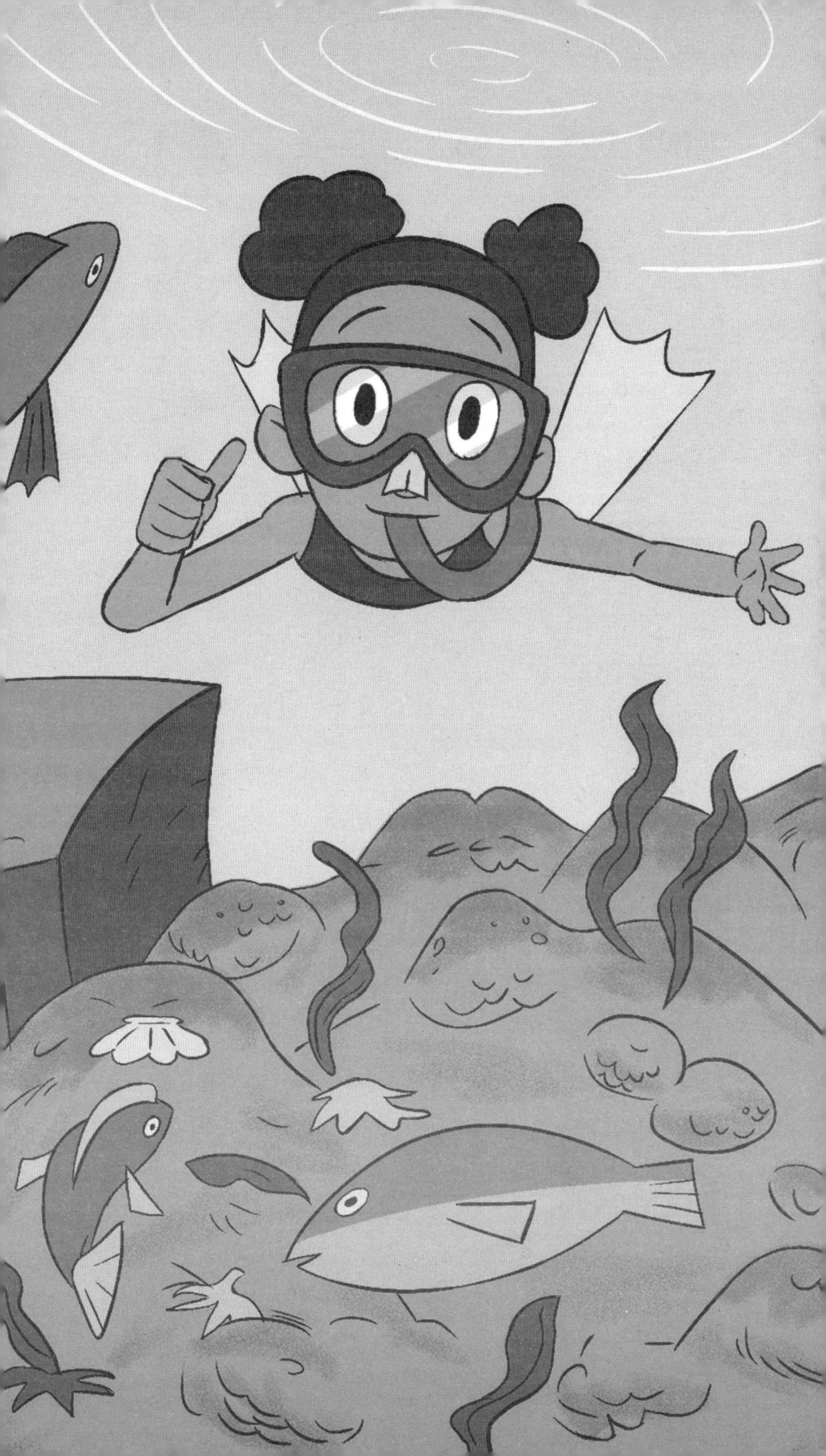

OPTION TWO: You buy a completely new wardrobe – everything that's been on your wish list for the last couple of years. Every day when you get dressed, you feel like the best version of yourself – it helps to know how hard you worked to earn this. It's the wardrobe of your dreams and you're Paris Fashion Week ready.

OPTION THREE: You and all of your friends go away for *the* most epic weekend ever! You start with a stack of pancakes covered in bacon, syrup and whipped cream at a nearby posh hotel, then head off to a theme park for the VIP treatment. You skip to the front of every queue and get to ride your favourite rollercoasters over and over and over (I'm starting to feel sick . . .). You fill up on pizza and milkshakes before you go to see your favourite singer in concert. And the VIP treatment hasn't ended. You're at the very front of the show with an amazing view and you get to meet them afterwards, hang out and get all the merch you've ever wanted for free and signed!

Now I don't think you need Chen, Ash or Sam's advice here – or even mine. Because when it comes to enjoying yourself, there's no winning option, there's just the one that's right for you. Sometimes people can become so focused on their goal and work so hard that they forget to stop to enjoy their success. I think enjoying yourself is such an important thing to do. And it all comes back to *why* we make money in the first place (in addition to paying for essentials) – to add value to our own life and the lives of others. If it's all work, work, work, you lose the enjoyment and the benefits. So next time you've worked really hard at something – whether it was studying for exams at school, practising a skill you're learning or training for a sporting event – remember to stop, look at how far you've come and treat yourself. Sometimes even just imagining what you'll do when you reach your goal can help motivate you while you're on your way. So kick back for a minute and let your imagination go wild – how would you reward yourself for all of that hard work?

TIME TO MAKE YOUR MILLION

Right, I hope you're feeling relaxed and refreshed after your break because it's time to get back down to business and reach our next and final goal: £1,000,000! We've come a LONG way since we held that pound coin in the palm of our hand and **WE'VE LEARNED SO MUCH**. After paying your tax and £9k on having some well-deserved time off, you've got £420,000 in the bank. Now it's time to combine everything you know for the final push. But before that, I want to tell you about one last person who's seriously succeeded in the business game and who is a big personal inspiration to me.

JAY-Z

Jay-Z, an American rapper, record producer and entrepreneur, became a billionaire in 2019. That's right, a billionaire! That's A LOT of money! And how did he become a billionaire? Well, he had multiple streams of income of course! Let me explain.

Jay-Z first rose to fame as a rapper. He was a pretty big deal and achieved global success with his music. But rather than just sticking to one thing, he decided he had more to offer and created another stream of income. Just like Rihanna, he used the money that he earned as a musician and put it towards building another business. He created Roc Nation, the record label, and went on to sign many successful artists, including Rihanna, Shakira and J. Cole.

He also invested his money by buying lots of houses and art (paintings and sculptures can be worth a serious amount of money), investing in the streaming company Tidal (where users can listen to music and podcasts), buying shares in the taxi company Uber and purchasing a drinks company.

Now, the key thing that Jay-Z did was take the money he earned from each investment and spend the profits on a different type of business, whether that was through setting up a new business or buying shares in a company that already existed. Then, when that business started to make a profit, guess what he did next? That's right, he used the profits he'd made to invest in *another* type of business. And he hasn't stopped. Even now he continues to invest money he's made from successful businesses into new ones!

We can learn a lot from this method of investing. It's called **diversifying your portfolio**. It *can* be (but is not always) better to put your money into different types of businesses rather than focus on just one massive business. It means that if one of your businesses is not doing so well, your other businesses are hopefully thriving. It's the same idea that we looked at when we talked about buying shares.

For example, with Jay-Z, even if there is a time in the year when his drinks company makes less money, it won't matter too much if his record label signs an artist who makes loads of sales!

Like Jay-Z, most millionaires (and billionaires) will have a diverse portfolio, which means they earn money from multiple streams of income. In fact, people say that the average millionaire has seven streams of income!

But that's just one way to get there. How are you going to finish the game? Now think about all that you have learned on this journey so far and choose wisely.

YOUR THREE OPTIONS

OPTION ONE: You're going back to your roots and investing in your car-washing business big time. When you were researching new companies to invest in, you found a very interesting car-washing business for sale. It costs £100,000 – that would mean spending around 24 per cent of your money investing in this new business. Up until now, you've been washing cars by hand, but this company owns machines that wash the cars for you (no more wrinkly fingers!). And it means you can wash many more cars at the same time. This makes you think it's worth the money and would be a wise investment. You decide to buy it and use £40,000 of your cash to hire two people to help run the business. Over time, once the profits start rolling in, you plan to use this money to set up car washes in new locations (at a slow pace – yeah, I'm looking at you, Spotify) and upgrade the equipment.

Sam

> This is the one I'd go for. Get back to what you really know, what you're really good at – washing cars. After washing cars for years, you have met so many amazing people, cleaned some stellar rides and honed your craft. Why not use that and invest in what you know?

SO, YOU WANT TO BE A MILLIONAIRE?

OPTION TWO: You know what, the private island life was a little too good and you've decided to tap out of this business world. You've learned loads and now it's time to enjoy yourself a little more and spend your hard-earned money. And you know exactly what you're going to do with it – wait until you turn seventeen and buy a Lamborghini in lime green! Learning to drive never looked so good! Having spent around £200,000 on the car, you'll still have loads of money left in the bank (£420,000 - £200,000 = £220,000) so you might get back into the investment game one day in the future. But for now it's chill time.

Ash

> Oh my days, a lambo – the dream! Yes, I'd kick it and retire in style. No shame there. You've worked hard and earned loads of money, but you must be tired, man. I'd totally call it a day, for now . . .

OPTION THREE: You're going to use all of the knowledge you've gained and diversify your portfolio. You use the money you've made to get back on the property ladder and buy two three-bedroom flats for £75,000 a piece, renting out each room for an affordable rate of £400 per month. You also spend £25,000 buying more shares on the stock market. And let's not forget the car wash – you're expanding to a second location.

It'll cost you £65 to set up the new site if you head back to your trusted wholesaler and £160 a month to employ someone to wash the cars. After spending that £65 in the first month to get things moving, you'll be bringing in £1,840 a month (£1,000 (per car wash) x 2 = £2,000. £2,000 - £160 (wages) = £1,840). And last but not least, you're going to invest the maximum amount you can for the year in an ISA (£20,000) and Premium Bonds (£50,000) so your money can start working for you. Phew, you've just spent almost £250,000 - that's almost half your cash (£75,000 (per flat) x 2 = £150,000. £150,000 + £25,000 (shares) + £225 (car-washing set-up cost + one month's wages) + £20,000 (ISA) + £50,000 (Premium Bonds) = £245,225). It might not be seven streams of income, but it's a really good start.

Chen

> You've come so far and I'm hooked. It'd all be about diversifying for me. You must be feeling so confident with all your finance skills, Eman is going to be out of a job. Stand back, people, you're about to become a millionaire!

SO, YOU WANT TO BE A MILLIONAIRE?

EMAN'S ADVICE

Do you know what? After all our time together, it's getting harder and harder to think of advice to give you! You're really learning and making smart choices as you go. I don't think you even need me to tell you what option I'd go for any more, you probably already know!
But for old times' sake, let's look at the upsides and downsides of the options.

OPTION ONE

Investing in yourself – I'm here for it. It's a wise choice. You started small, but you've gained knowledge, experience and loyal customers, and this option allows you to build on that now. Plus by investing in your *own* business (rather than buying shares in someone else's), you'll make more money when it does well, meaning you'll potentially get to £1 million quicker. And for anyone who is still doubting whether there's money to be made in car-related things, let me quickly tell you about the Issa brothers, Mohsin and Zuber.

MOHSIN AND ZUBER ISSA

In 2001, Mohsin and Zuber Issa owned a single petrol station near Manchester. But as other petrol stations were being put up for sale by big oil companies, they saw an opportunity and started buying lots of these petrol stations around the country, growing their business. And rather than just selling petrol, they started selling other things too, such as coffee, fast food and groceries. Over the next twenty years their business grew and grew and grew, thanks to all of the petrol stations they'd bought and the extra products they were selling. **IN FACT, TODAY THEY ARE BOTH BILLIONAIRES!** So don't doubt what you can achieve with just a single car-washing business.

But there are always downsides to expanding, and you need to make sure this new car-washing company is as good as the current owners say it is. For example, you might buy the business only to find out half of the machines are broken or they stretched the truth about how many customers they get each month. There are some risks, but as long as you do the research and the work, it's a great option to reach £1 million. And if you keep growing your business, why stop at £1 million? Be inspired by the Issa brothers and keep going!

OPTION TWO

Personally, I like to finish what I started, but this isn't my choice, it's yours, and I'm going to respect that you've worked hard and put in a lot of time and effort. If you feel it's time to end your journey then I understand your decision. You know yourself best. Plus you're going to have a flash car and I can get on board with a Lamborghini - although lime green, what are you thinking? Classic yellow is more my style.

OPTION THREE

OK, we've already talked a lot about the pros of diversifying your portfolio, so let's start with the cons here. The main worry is that having so many different streams of income takes a lot of time to manage properly. You'll now need to make sure both your car-washing sites are running smoothly. You'll also need to make sure your tenants are happy *and* you're keeping on top of collecting rent and managing property repairs.

Not to mention checking the stock market regularly to see how your shares are doing – are they increasing in value or decreasing? Do you need to take your money out and invest it elsewhere? And remember to keep an eye on those interest rates for your ISA too – is there another bank offering better rates that you should move your money to?

With all that being said, I trust you'll be able to do this. You've learned loads, you're committed to the goal and we've seen that this method is a great way to earn a lot of money, without relying on just one stream of income. You have a great chance of meeting your £1 million goal with this option, and maybe even going beyond it.

EMAN'S PICK

I'm hanging up my navy-blue baseball cap! I think you've learned everything I have to teach you. If you call it a day with option two, I respect your decision – it's not my place to tell you what you should or shouldn't do with your time. I told you how important your time is, right at the start of the game. Don't forget that! And as for options one and three, both are strong investment ideas, and both have the potential to get you to the goal of a million pounds.

SO, YOU WANT TO BE A MILLIONAIRE?

You see, there's never only one route to making money – if it was that simple, we'd all be doing it and sitting comfortably with millions in the bank. But it's not. However, with the knowledge and skills you've learned on our journey together, I hope you'll now feel more confident about going out into the world, understanding your options, judging the risks carefully and making smart choices.

So I guess what I'm saying is that my final pick is you!

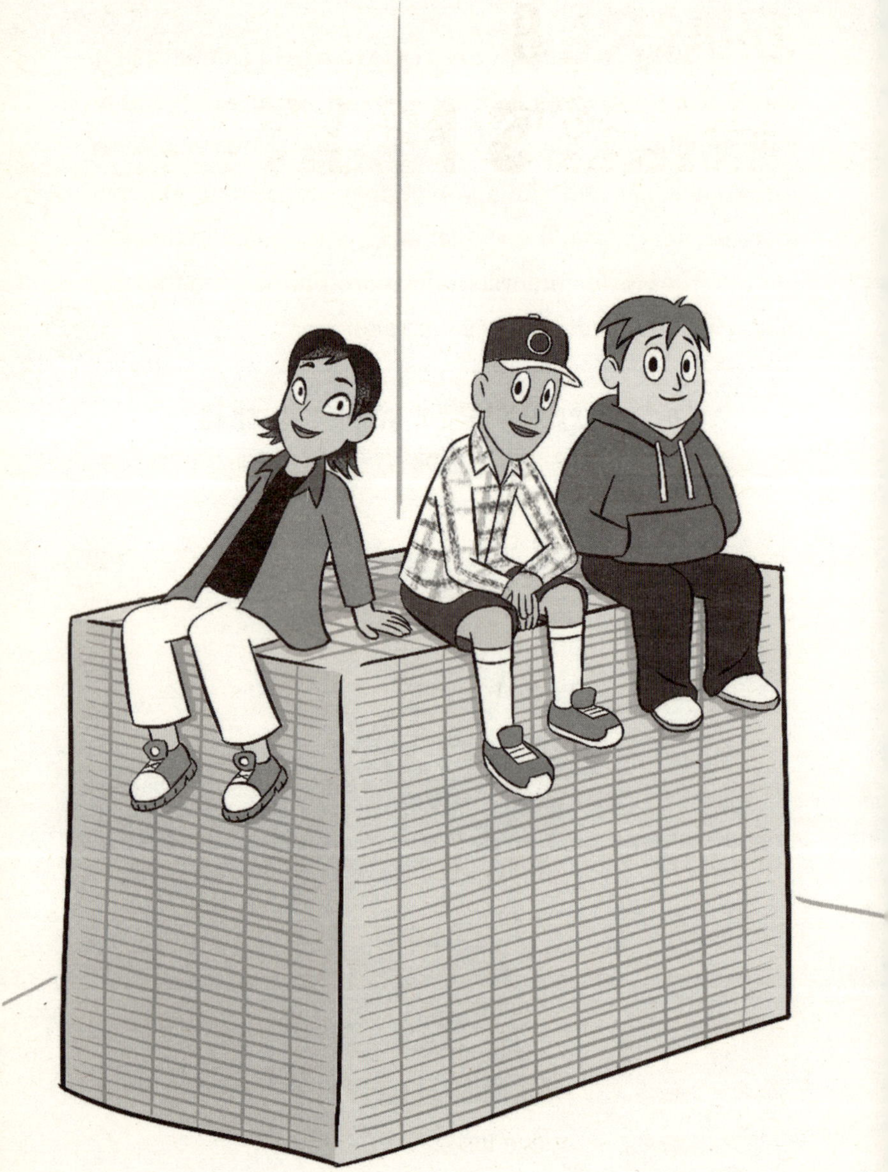

CHAPTER 8
WHAT'S NEXT?

KLAXON ALERT

CONGRATULATIONS! YOU MADE £1,000,000.

(Or maybe not, if you caved in and bought that Lambo!) But for the rest of you, you stayed focused on your goal, put in the work and built an incredible tree of wealth that will continue to grow for years and years.

Now that you have reached your financial goal, I want to take you back to the very beginning of the book. We touched on the importance of giving back and I suggested donating 10 per cent of your money to a cause that matters to you (see page 24). Well, that's what this chapter is all about. We won't be talking about how you can make even more money; hopefully this book has given you the tools you need to do that already. Instead, I want to take a moment to explain *why* I believe it's so important to share what we have with others.

Money plays such an important role in our lives. We all deserve to live comfortably and enjoy life to the fullest. That's why I wanted to teach you how to make money and build wealth – to make sure you live a full and happy life. But as well as creating a better life for ourselves, it's also important to help others along the way.

No matter how much money you have, there is always someone with less than you. We've all been in a situation in life where we've needed a helping hand, even if it's not with money. Maybe someone helped you with your homework, or a friend's parent gave you a lift to an event you were going to, or your family paid for you to go on a day trip with your school. Most of us know how it feels to need help from others, in one way or another. And we know how much better it can feel once you've received the help you needed. This is why I believe that, whenever we can, we should give something back to those who are in need.

I GIVE AWAY 10 PER CENT OF MY SALARY EVERY MONTH.

Sometimes to charities, or specific causes or people. As well as helping out my mum, I've also donated to orphanages in Nigeria and Uganda. I've been sent pictures from the charity that show how the money is being used to help children, and it feels amazing to know that I've contributed to that. When I can, I try to donate more, but 10 per cent is my minimum. That won't be something that everyone can afford, and that's fine. People can decide based on their own situations what they can give.

WHAT'S NEXT?

But remember, giving back doesn't always have to be financial. You may not be able to help people with money, but you might be able to volunteer in a care home or community centre. Or you can give food to food banks and clothes to charity shops.

Of course I still enjoy treating myself to things, and there's nothing wrong with that, but knowing that I've put some money aside to have a positive impact on someone else's life is priceless.

> **Helping others is a reward that money just can't buy.**

MARCUS RASHFORD

The footballer Marcus Rashford was born in Manchester in a single-parent household, and his mother had to work multiple jobs to provide for him and his siblings. Sometimes his mother would have to skip meals so there was enough food for her children. It was a difficult time for Marcus, but he soon went on to become a **SUPER-SUCCESSFUL FOOTBALL PLAYER** for Manchester United.

However, even after his rise to fame, he never forgot about where he came from and the challenges his family had faced. He has used his position as a famous footballer to help disadvantaged children across the country.

In 2020, when the world was in lockdown due to the Covid-19 pandemic, Marcus became concerned that many children in poorer families would not be able to eat because their main meals normally came from having free school dinners, and schools were closed for most children. Marcus donated money to help provide these children with meals. And then he used his voice to encourage other people to donate money too. He raised an incredible £20 million, and this money provided 3 million meals for children across the UK. **INSPIRING, RIGHT?**

But it doesn't stop there. Marcus also set up a charity called the End Child Food Poverty Taskforce, which has worked with various cafes and supermarkets to provide free meals and food vouchers for children. I respect Marcus a lot – once he had made it as a football star, he reflected on his own experiences and chose to give back to his community and country. **THAT'S WHAT IT'S ALL ABOUT.**

PRIYANKA CHOPRA JONAS

Here's another great example. Bollywood and Hollywood actress Priyanka Chopra Jonas has also used her wealth and success to help others. As an Indian immigrant growing up in the USA, teenage Priyanka experienced racism, and it made her question her self-worth. There were many times as a child when she didn't believe in herself.

She refused to be defeated by this though. She decided that whenever she walked into a room, even if she was really scared and nervous, she would tell herself she wasn't afraid and act as confidently as possible. And it worked. People started to believe she was that confident and, eventually, she started to feel that confidence in herself too!

She's passionate about passing this on to other girls and women, making sure that they too have self-belief. She thinks that education is an important way to do this. So, she set up a foundation that helps pay for an education for people in need. She has helped more than fifty girls and young women in India who come from underprivileged backgrounds to get an education.

WHAT'S NEXT?

Priyanka believes that without this, girls end up having to rely on other people to help them. But with an education, they can make their own decisions, lead a life that is right for them and feel more confident.

Priyanka is also a Global Goodwill Ambassador for the charity UNICEF, who help improve the lives of children in more than 190 countries around the world. Since 2016, she has used her time and her voice to help raise awareness about the importance of education for girls.

It's not just her time that she gives, though. It's also reported that she donates 10 per cent of her earnings **(CLEARLY TAKING TIPS FROM ME!)** each year to her foundation. She says, 'You just have to look around you and ask, "What little bit can I do? Whose life can I touch?"' and I couldn't put it better myself. It's not about the big gestures, but the little things we all do to make the world a better place.

Is there anyone whom you could help with your time or money? Is there an issue in your community that you are passionate about and want to change? Take a moment to think about how just 10 per cent of your money – that's £100,000 (£1,000,000 ÷ 100 (per cent) = £10,000. £10,000 x 10 (per cent) = £100,000) or £22,000 if you went with option two in the last chapter (£220,000 ÷ 100 (per cent) = £2,200. £2,200 x 10 (per cent) = £22,000) – could make a difference to the lives of others.

THE ULTIMATE GUIDE TO MONEY

I'm not going to tell you what to do any more though! You have made a life-changing amount of money in this game, and what you do with it is your choice. What do *you* want to do next?

Ash: I must admit, the Money Man is right. One mill is a lot of cash and you could spend it all on yourself, but it would be pretty cool to help others out too.

Chen: Yeah, I agree. Before, I would have said, 'Put it all in a savings account!' but I like this 50-40-10 rule. You can give 10 per cent to help a cause you care about. I remember my teacher talking about how many children live in poverty around the world, and she mentioned a charity that helps by providing food and other things they need. I think that would be a good cause to give to.

Sam: That's a great idea, Chen! I've been thinking about the many people in the country who don't have a home. Maybe you could give your 10 per cent to a homeless shelter.

WHAT'S NEXT?

Ash

And you can also help by donating your time too. There's a summer fair at my local community centre soon to raise money for charity. Maybe you could help run a stall if there's something like that near you?

Yeah, let's do it!

Chen

Sam

BUY FLOWERS FOR MUM
INVEST IN HOBBY
SING IN PUBLIC
RAISE £1000
LEARN GREEK
BUY DAD A WATCH
DO HOMEWORK
BAKE A CAKE
OPEN ISA
SAVE UP FOR DRIVING LESSONS
BE NICER TO SISTER
GO FOR A JOG
DONATE TO CHARITY
SAVE FOR UNI

CONCLUSION

What a journey! And we've finally made it to the end! Woohoo! We've done it – whether you turned that one pound into a million or several thousand of them, you've learned how to spend wisely, how best to invest in yourself and about the power of giving back. These are all lessons that can be used to bring more value to your life and the lives of those around you.

As the game comes to an end and we leave Eman's fantasy finance world, there are three lessons I'd love for you to take with you into the real world. They're not only to do with money. Instead, these are bigger lessons about how you live your life, because I want you to achieve amazing things that bring you happiness.

1. FOCUS ON YOUR GOAL. Try to always keep the goal you're trying to achieve at the front of your mind. Maybe write it down on a Post-it note and put it on your mirror! This could be a small goal, such as staying on top of your homework during the week so that you have time to play all weekend, or a big goal, such as identifying and working towards what you want to do when you grow up. Either way, there is great power in finding the thing that motivates you, staying focused and going after your dreams.

And when you're tempted to take a shortcut, think back to what we've discussed about instant gratification versus delayed gratification. Deciding between whether you should pick something that you're going to benefit from immediately or wait for an even greater reward can be challenging; even I still struggle with it sometimes.

There will be times in life when you work hard without seeing the benefits straight away, which will be a frustrating and perhaps even disappointing experience. But I hope our journey together has shown you how disappointments and mistakes are all part of the process. Sometimes you have to patiently wait for the seeds of your work to grow, but it's worth it in the end. So many success stories share these difficult experiences and I want to encourage you to always remember that greatness takes time and focus. There is power in being patient!

2. BELIEVE IN YOURSELF. I've given you a lot of advice in this book, and told you what my choices would be, but I don't always know what the best decision is for you – only *you* know that. So I want you to believe in yourself, even if sometimes you feel like you aren't good enough or that you want to give up on your dream. You're so special. We all are. And we all have something to offer this world. So follow your own path and trust yourself to create the life that's right for you.

CONCLUSION

3. BALANCE. I know I've talked a lot about pushing towards the goal of a million pounds and staying focused, but really the best thing to do is to keep a healthy balance. Work hard, yes, but also take a break when you need to. Sometimes the magic happens when you're still and your mind is clear. Reward yourself with the things you like; you deserve to enjoy the amazing things life brings.

OK, THOSE ARE MY FINAL LESSONS. I've shared nearly all of my wisdom with you (aren't you lucky!). Now you're in the driver's seat, and it's time to take what you've learned and begin making smart choices with your money and your life. You can't do everything at once, so take one step at a time. Use this book as a guide and refer back to it whenever you need it. Think about what lesson you want to try out first. Perhaps you have a skill that you want to try to turn into a business? Maybe, when that business starts making a profit, you want to focus on using the 50-40-10 rule? Whatever you choose, well done for taking those first steps.

> I can't wait to see the amazing things you do. Good luck!

GLOSSARY

advertise – a way to promote a service or product that is being sold. Word-of-mouth and leaflets are ways of advertising.

bank account – a place where people keep their money. It's like a file that records how much money a person has saved with or borrowed from a bank.

bankruptcy – when the amount of money someone owes is more than the amount of money they have.

barter – exchanging goods or services for other goods or services, rather than paying for them with money.

blockchain – a digital graph that lists all the things someone has bought with a cryptocurrency.

budget – a money plan. It shows someone how much money they have, how much they need, how much they will spend and how much they will have left at the end.

capital gains tax – a type of direct tax. It is paid to the government in the UK when someone sells something that has increased in value, such as a second home or shares.

cost of living crisis – a situation where people have less money for things that they need than they did a couple of years ago. It is caused by the cost of everyday items going up, while people's earnings are not increasing at the same rate.

credit cards – a credit card can be a simple and flexible way to spend money borrowed from a bank or lender, which you will then be given options on how to repay.

cryptocurrency – a digital form of money that is created by computer code. It can't be touched or used in the physical world.

current account – a type of bank account where people tend to keep money for the things they pay for regularly, such as bus or train tickets, food, clothes, going out with friends and hobbies.

delayed gratification – when someone resists the temptation to spend their money straight away so that they can enjoy a reward in the future.

demand – how much people want a product or service.

deposit – an amount of money paid by someone to confirm that they want to buy something, such as a house. A deposit is usually a percentage of the total cost of the thing they are looking to buy.

direct tax – money taken directly from a person or business's salary that goes straight to a government to be spent on public services.

distribution – the process of making a product or service available for the consumer or business user who needs it.

diversifying your portfolio – when someone invests their money into several different types of business. They do this to increase their chances of making money and lower their risk of losing money if one business performs badly.

dividend – money received by someone who owns part of a company.

early exit fee – a charge you pay if you pay off a loan or close an investment before an agreed contracted time. Not all lenders or investment companies charge this fee and you should be made aware of this charge before you agree to the financial product.

economy – the way that people spend and make money, which is usually by either selling or buying products or services.

economy of scale – the more of an item that is made, bought or sold, the cheaper it becomes.

finance – the management of money. It includes activities such as investing, borrowing, lending, budgeting, saving and forecasting.

financial advisor – someone who gives people advice about how to make good choices with their money.

forgery – when someone produces a fake version of something, such as money or a painting, and pretends it's the original item.

gambling – when someone spends a certain amount of money on something and hopes to get more money in return, even though there is a risk they could lose their money.

high-risk investment – when the possibility of making or losing lots of money through investing is high.

immediate gratification – the instant happy feeling someone gets when they spend money on something they want as soon as they see it.

income tax – a tax set by and paid to governments on income or profits earned by individuals or companies.

indirect tax – a fee added to products people buy. It goes from the customer to the government via someone else, such as a supplier. The government then spends it on public services.

inflation – how much the price of an item increases or decreases over time.

interest – an amount, or percentage, of money. It can be given to someone as a reward for saving their money or added on top of money borrowed as a fee.

interest rate – an interest rate tells you how high the cost of borrowing is, or how high the rewards are for saving.

investment – something someone buys or puts money into that they believe will increase in worth over time, making them more money than they started with.

ISA – an Individual Savings Account. A place where someone saves money and receives interest on those savings that isn't taxed. Between £1 and £20,000 can be put into an ISA each year.

JISA – a Junior Individual Savings Account. A place where anyone under the age of eighteen can save money. They will receive tax-free interest on those savings. Up to £9,000 a year can be put into a JISA.

loan – a fixed amount of money that someone borrows, often from a bank, and has agreed to pay back.

lodger – a person who pays to live in a spare bedroom of someone else's house.

lottery – a game of luck where winners get selected through a random drawing of numbers.

low-risk investment – when the possibility of making or losing lots of money through investing is low.

mortgage – the money borrowed, usually from a bank, to pay for a building such as a house. It is paid back over a number of years by the borrower and includes a fee for borrowing the money.

NFT (non-fungible tokens) – a type of cryptocurrency, which is represented by a digital image that is one-of-a-kind and can't be copied or stolen.

platform – an app or website where someone can buy or sell shares.

Premium Bond – a place where someone saves money. Each month their money is entered into a draw where they have the chance of winning money as a prize.

profit – the money that is made when someone sells something for more than it cost them.

property – a building, such as a house or a flat, that belongs to someone.

regulated – when a company is investigated to make sure they are telling the truth about how much money they make.

rent – the money owed by someone living in or using a building. It is usually paid monthly to the person who owns the building.

repossession – when a bank or lender takes items that someone owns because they haven't paid back the money that they borrowed. The items taken add up to the value of money borrowed, plus interest and fines.

savings – the amount of money left over after someone has paid for everything they need or want. This money is usually put to one side in a piggy bank or bank account and not spent very often.

savings account – a place where someone keeps the money that they don't plan to spend very often.

share – a part of a company that you can buy and own.

shareholder – the name for people who have bought part of a company.

side hustle – the work or a job someone does on top of their day-to-day life or another career, in order to increase their income.

solicitor – a legal professional who provides legal advice to clients.

start-up – a newly set-up business.

stock market – the place where shares are bought and sold.

stockbroker – a person who buys and sells shares for other people.

stocks and shares ISA – a tax-efficient investment account. This means you don't have to pay UK income tax or capital gains tax on money you earn from your investments made through the ISA.

stream of income – the different ways in which a business owner or individual can earn money.

supply – the amount of a product that is available.

target market – the people who are suited to a particular product and are most likely to buy it.

tax – an amount of money that workers and businesses must pay to a government. It is used to pay for public services, such as hospitals, schools and rubbish collection.

tenant – a person who pays to live in a building, such as a house, that is owned by someone else.

unregulated – when a company is not investigated to make sure they are telling the truth about how much money they make.

Value Added Tax – a type of indirect tax. It is added to goods and services in the UK and the money goes to the government to pay for public services.

wages – payment made by an employer to an employee for work done in a specific period of time.

wholesaler – a company that sells products in large quantities, or bulk, which lowers the cost per item.